DONALD TRUMP

IN THE FOOTSTEPS OF ADOLF HITLER

THE DANGEROUS PARALLELS BETWEEN TRUMP
AND HISTORICAL DICTATORS

A EUROPEAN'S PERSPECTIVE

GEIR SIVERTSEN

Book Title: Donald Trump In The Footsteps Of Adolf Hitler

Written by Geir Sivertsen

Book cover by 100 Covers.

ISBN 978-82-693751-1-4

https://gewibooks.com

CONTENTS

Patriotism means to stand by the country, not by the President."
—President Theodore Roosevelt

DONALD TRUMP

IN THE FOOTSTEPS OF ADOLF HITLER

DONALD TRUMP. THE BIGGEST THREAT TO AMERICAN DEMOCRACY SINCE THE CIVIL WAR

As a retired European who has spent 25 years studying and working in various countries and cultures, including a year in the U.S., I believe my unique perspective on American politics and history allows me to notice what many Americans overlook. I want to share my insights on why Donald Trump is more dangerous than many in the United States seem to realize. Below is an edited version of my notes, starting from when Donald Trump made his unconventional approach to Kim Jong-un in North Korea. I found it intriguing, observing his straightforward approach to such a complex issue. With my background as a business manager, I was drawn to the idea of a businessman as president—perhaps not such a bad idea?

However, it didn't take long for me to see Donald Trump's *"true colors."* His colors are only black and white, revealing an ego-centered person marked by narcissism, hatred, and an unwillingness to compromise.

In the following observations, I hope to shed light on these true colors.

Donald Trump—a dangerous man for American democracy.

Donald Trump has transformed a popular reality TV figure into an aspiring authoritarian with Hitler-like traits, bringing the United States close to its breaking point. A government that, until very recently, was considered "the Beacon of Democracy."[1]

How can such a man be described? Let me describe Donald Trump from my European perspective, using facts, his statements, and the opinions of others.

Examining his personality, background, achievements, and failures, it becomes clear how the combination of his political tactics, Hitler-like charisma in rallies, extensive use of lies and threats, along with the support of power-hungry and intimidated Republican leaders and cunning collaborators, propelled him to the pinnacle of the American political hierarchy.

Core issues in the upcoming 2024 presidential election.

The political landscape in the upcoming presidential election is nearly as divided as before the Civil War 200 years ago. However, unlike that time, the main issue driving division today is not slavery. Here are the key issues:

- Economy: The American economy remains relatively unaffected by the president's identity, but the growing wealth gap has become intolerable. Essential needs like access to healthcare are at risk, with differing approaches from the Republican and Democratic Parties. Job creation, historically, has seen little impact from partisan politics.
- Abortion rights: Should women have the right to decide within certain limits or no rights at all?
- Voting rights: Should people's voting rights be restricted or expanded?
- Influence in courts: Which political party should have increased influence in national and local courts?
- Climate: Should the focus be on short-term local economic gain or long-term climate improvement? The real question is: What kind of climate do we want for our children?
- Immigration: Should there be a hardline approach or a more lenient one? The significant number of illegal immigrants fleeing poverty and conflict zones has made this a primary concern. Donald Trump takes a hardline stance with clear elements of racism, advocating for sealing the border with a solid wall. Democrats propose increased funding to enhance and manage border control.
- Gun control: The U.S. has a long-standing tradition and constitutional protection that allows citizens to own guns. It is now the country with the highest gun ownership and among the countries with the easiest gun laws in the world. Result:

Gun violence and gun deaths are significantly higher per capita than in any other industrialized country in the world.

There are basically two diametrically opposed viewpoints. One, with particularly firm support in rural areas, is that having a gun is part of the freedom of individual rights, protected specifically by the Constitution. The opposing view, with the strongest support in urban areas, is that better and tighter control of who can bear firearms will decrease gun-related violence and deaths.

The Republican Party and the Democratic Party stand on opposite sides of these issues, and the stakes are high. However, despite the critical nature of these issues, many Americans are not particularly enthusiastic about this election. Both presidential candidates are elderly and show signs of cognitive decline. The memory of the January 6 insurrection is fading as daily struggles take precedence. Grocery prices are at record highs, challenging essentials like gas and insurance. Many are working multiple jobs to make ends meet, which leaves little time or energy for political engagement.

For some, the decision may be whether life felt easier during Trump's presidency. Trump excelled at promoting the idea that *"the economy was the greatest in the world"* during his tenure. Still, the overall economic reality is less rosy, with widening income and wealth gaps hitting middle and low-income families hardest. Neither party has effectively addressed this issue.

Looking beyond these challenges, voters must critically assess who Trump truly is. My advice is to focus on facts rather than falsehoods and promises. It's important not to dismiss Trump supporters; they have their reasons. However, I will demonstrate how Trump is intoxicating the political atmosphere and seriously threatening American democracy and why a second term could jeopardize individual rights.

In conclusion, Trump appears consumed by power, resembling dictators worldwide. **Is this the leader America truly wants?**

CHAPTER 1

TRUMP, IN THE FOOTSTEPS OF ADOLF HITLER

Is it unfair to compare Trump with Hitler?

D onald J. Trump, born on June 14, 1946, has undergone a remarkable transformation in just a few years—from a charismatic but unpredictable leader to someone who stops at nothing to achieve his personal, and some would say the fanatical, goal of regaining presidential power. After four years of research for this book, it has become increasingly clear, with each passing day, that Donald Trump and an intimidated Republican Party leadership are steering America down a problematic path. From a European perspective, the political situation in the U.S. is starting to bear a troubling resemblance to Hitler's rise to power in Germany a century ago.

Donald Trump is acting dangerously close to how Hitler operated in Germany preceding WWII, and the Republican Party, almost entirely in the hands of Trump, is accepting political views that more and more resemble fascism/neofascism.[2][3] (Neo-fascism is a post-World War II ideology rooted in the same core values as Fascism/Nazism but adapted for different geographical and cultural contexts.) But wait—am I suggesting that under the leadership of Donald Trump, the Republican Party resembles a neo-fascist party? Isn't that an overreaction?

Consider the following facts. Below are core fascistic values, with the first six vigorously pursued by Trump and many Republican leaders, while the remaining six are wholly or partly embraced by the GOP:

1. Authoritarian ambitions, advocating for one strong leader and one strong party.
2. Strong nationalism.
3. Populism that appeals to ordinary people who feel neglected by established elite groups, framing it as *"the people"* against *"the elite."*
4. Embracing violence to suppress opposition, even through force if necessary.
5. Advocating for mass mobilization.
6. Opposition to parliamentary democracy.
7. Xenophobia: Demonstrating dislike or prejudice against people from other countries.
8. Anti-immigration policies.
9. Promotion of racial supremacy.
10. Endorsement of conservative, right-wing economic programs that favor the wealthy.
11. Opposition to *"the left,"* ranging from communists to democratic socialists.
12. Rejection of political and cultural liberalism.

This shift toward an ideology rooted in fascism cannot occur without the encouragement and acceptance of leadership, in this case from Donald Trump and his Republican allies. This alignment becomes even more apparent when examining the parallels between Donald Trump, who has led the GOP for the past six years, and one of the most notorious and dangerous fascists in modern history—German dictator Adolf Hitler.

Let's delve into the key points.

Hitler and Trump similarities:[4]

1. Both were ridiculed and underestimated.
2. Both utilize a Big Lie as a foundation.
3. Propagation of a barrage of falsehoods.
4. Promoting slogans like *"Make our country great again"* to evoke patriotism.
5. Leveraging their personalities as charismatic leaders.
6. Exhibiting qualities of great demagogues.
7. Engaging in hateful and harassing rhetoric.
8. Habitually shifting blame onto others.
9. Demonstrating racist tendencies.
10. Engaging in tax evasion.
11. Displaying contempt for the law.
12. Pardoning criminals who aided their causes.
13. Garnering support from business magnates.
14. Surrounding themselves with a criminal entourage.
15. Participating in failed attempts to seize power illegitimately.

16. Encouraging supporter violence against targeted victims.

It is scary, almost beyond imagination, that a description of Adolf Hitler fits so perfectly with Donald Trump of today.

Philip Rucker and Carol Leonnig, co-authors of the book *"I Alone Can Fix It,"* remarked:

> *"It would have been unfathomable to liken an American president to Adolf Hitler. Consider the vastly different histories of Nazi Germany and the United States and the divergent paths these countries have taken. Yet, here we are in the 21st century, in the year 2020, witnessing an American president exhibiting authoritarian impulses, rhetoric, and behavior reminiscent of Adolf Hitler. It's truly remarkable and, quite frankly, unbelievable."*

Four years later, what was once unbelievable has become evident. Below, I elaborate on the sixteen points previously mentioned, starting with things that, on the surface issues, may seem troublesome but are easy to overlook; however, as the list progresses, you'll observe someone who believes he is above the law and beyond democratic accountability.

Before delving into the point-by-point comparison, let me briefly explain how Adolf Hitler, a World War I soldier, ascended to leadership in Germany and initiated another catastrophic World War. Born in 1889, Hitler took his own life in 1945 following Germany's total defeat.

His upbringing was marred by harsh relations with his father, who was sometimes brutal, though he had a close bond with his mother until her death when Hitler was 17. After a period adrift in Munich, he volunteered for the German army and served throughout the war from 1914 to 1918.

Disillusioned after the war, Hitler found allies among those disenchanted with the post-war democratic society. Germany was devastated by the conflict, suffering heavy casualties and widespread material damage. The Treaty of Versailles imposed harsh conditions on Germany, hindering economic recovery. Various political parties, including the Communists, attempted to govern in the years following the war. Germany's post-WWI situation was economically dire and politically unstable—ideal conditions for a demagogue to challenge the establishment.

Hitler, with extreme demagogic power, organizational talent, and dedicated collaborators like Goebbels, Goring, and Himmler, maneuvered to the top through threats and political cunning. Once in power, he violently suppressed opposition and launched a crusade to avenge Germany's humiliation in World War I. Blaming Jews and Communists, he initiated mass deportations to concentration camps and pursued territorial expansion through military aggression against other nations, sparking World War II.

Let's closely examine the facts.

1. Both were ridiculed and underestimated.

Hitler:

Hitler was widely ridiculed before coming to power, and in the years leading up to Hitler's ascent as chancellor and dictator, political opponents and intellectuals disparaged him, labeling him a *"half-insane rascal,"* a *"pathetic dunderhead,"* a *"nowhere fool,"* a *"big mouth,"* a self-obsessed *"clown,"* and an egomaniac who loved only himself.

However, after Hitler and the Nazi Party seized power, joking or ridiculing Hitler became perilous. For instance, Marianna Kürchner, an employee at an ammunition factory, was executed by guillotine in June 1943 for cracking a joke: Hitler and Göring stand atop a Berlin tower, and Hitler expresses a desire to do something to bring smiles to Berliners' faces. Göring responds, *"Why don't you jump?"*

(Note: There is a similar joke about Trump in an airplane; I will refrain from sharing it here.)

Hitler was vastly underestimated both in Germany for the cruelty to come and internationally for his war plans:

In Germany, before he came to power, few could imagine his *"no mercy"* policy after becoming Germany's leader and dictator in 1933.

Internationally, despite his aggressive expansion by force, Western European leaders placed faith in his repeated assurances of peaceful intentions—until he attacked England.

"As far as Hitler's long-term wishes were concerned, his con-servative coalition partners believed either that he was not serious or that they could exert a moderating influence on him. In any case, they were severely mistaken."[5]

Trump:

Trump has been likened to Hitler and subjected to similar ridicule, with nicknames such as *"Drumpf," "A pimple in the butt," "Trumpanzee," "malignant narcissist," "mob boss," "incompetent," "arrogant," "idiot," "egotistical," "igno-rant,"* and more. Jokes like *"What's the difference between a Trump and a flying pig?" "The letter F"* also reflects the sentiments of many.

Of course, modern leaders often attract nicknames, whether deserved or not. However, with Hitler and Trump, these nicknames seem to resonate deeply with many. Supporters, on the other hand, characterize them positively as *"strong," "charismatic," "the leader we need,"* and so forth.

History has clearly defined Adolf Hitler's character-istics. Time will reveal which characteristics best describe Donald Trump.

Trump was underestimated as a presidential candidate in 2016, and started his 'election stolen' campaign after his electoral defeat in 2020. His authoritarian plans for a potential second term 2024 should be taken seriously. Despite numerous warnings, 40% of Americans believe America would be better off with Trump.

2. "The Big Lie."

Hitler:

Hitler blamed Germany's weaknesses on the influence of Jewish and communist minorities, accusing them of plotting to seize control of the country. In a speech to a Munich audience in 1922, he asserted, *"There are only two possibilities: Either victory of the Aryan, or annihilation of the Aryan and the victory of the Jew."* This rhetoric marked the beginning of the Jewish extermination program. However, convincing Germans of this narrative posed a challenge, as Jews were well-integrated into German society and enjoyed positive local relationships across the country. The solution? The use of a repetitive *"big lie,"* a concept Hitler described in his 1925 book *"Mein Kampf"* (written in prison).

Hitler wrote: *"...in the big lie, there is always a certain force of credibility because the broad masses of a nation are always more easily corrupted in the deeper strata of their emotional nature than consciously or voluntarily; and thus, in the primitive simplicity of their minds, they more readily fall victims to the big lie than the small lie, since they often tell small lies in little matters but would be ashamed to resort to large-scale falsehoods. It would never come into their heads to fabricate colossal untruths, and they would not believe that others could have the audacity to distort the truth so infamously. Even though the facts which prove this to be so may be brought clearly to their minds, they will still doubt and waver and will continue to think that there may be some other explanation."*

He also emphasized the necessity of popular and simplistic propaganda: *"All propaganda must be popular, and its intellectual level must be adjusted to the most limited intelligence among those it is addressed to. ... The receptivity of the great masses is very limited; their intelligence is small, but their power of forgetting is enormous. As a consequence of these facts, all effective propaganda must be limited to very few points and must harp on these in slogans until the last member of the public understands what you want him to understand by your slogan."*[6] [7]

In short:

"The broad mass of a nation...will more easily fall victim to a big lie than to a small one. If you keep repeating it, people will eventually come to believe it."

Neither Hitler nor Goebbels (Hitler's *"Minister for Public Enlightenment and Propaganda"*) ever admitted to lying but continuously emphasized the unfounded message that Jews and communists were the root of Germany's problems. While some may have believed this narrative, many did not. However, the *"Big Lie"* was a powerful tool to sway the German people.

Trump:

Influenced by strategists like Steve Bannon and Paul Manafort, Trump adopted a strategy reminiscent of Hitler's and Goebbels': repeated lying to convince people to believe falsehoods. *"The big election lie"* emerged after his 2020 presidential election loss and was reiterated persistently, leading a significant portion of the American populace to embrace Trump's claims—echoing how Germans believed Hitler nearly 90 years ago.

Consider how, in the months leading up to the election, President Trump cast doubt on the integrity of the United States electoral system. He asserted that mail-in voting was corrupt, alleged fraudulent counting at polling places, and suggested that any loss would be due to such corruption. These statements persuaded many Americans that his defeat in 2020 resulted from widespread transgression rather than a genuine loss.

Just as the repeated lies about Jews and Communists formed the foundation for Hitler's consolidation of power, Trump's persistent lies about election falsehoods underpinned his bid to reclaim the presidency.

3. A barrage of lies.

Hitler:

Hitler's *"Big Lie"* was merely one in a series of falsehoods. A former finance minister noted that *Hitler "was so thoroughly untruthful that he could no longer recognize the difference between lies and truth."*

The editors of one edition of *"Mein Kampf"* (written during his prison time in 1923 and later used extensively for Nazi propaganda) described it as *a "swamp of lies, distortions, half-truths, and real facts."* Lies became an integral part of Hitler's deceitful rhetoric and the Nazi propaganda machine.

Typically, when claimed by clever demagogues and amplified by the media of the day (radio, newspapers, films, and copious pamphlets), these lies morphed into *"political truths"*—truths that were not debunked until the end of WWII.

Here are some examples from *"Hitler's Lies: A Short Documented List of the More Conspicuous Lies of Adolf Hitler, from 1933 to 1943, in Chronological Order,"* issued by the Office of War Information on December 14, 1943. These examples primarily concern Hitler's proclaimed peaceful intentions and denial of war plans:

- Oct. 14, 1933: Announcing Germany's withdrawal from the League of Nations, Hitler's proclamation claimed, *"The National Cabinet disavows violence as an unsuitable means for settling differences with the European Community of States."*
- March 16, 1935: Explaining rearmament, Hitler's proclamation stated, *"…the German government affirms that it wishes in the National German armament to create no instrument for military aggression…"*
- Sept. 14, 1936, at Nuremberg: *"We, National Socialists, do not wish that our military resources should be employed to force on other peoples what those peoples themselves do not want."*
- Nov. 6, 1938, at Weimar: *"As a peace-loving man… all we desire is the right to live the same as other nations."*
- April 1, 1940, the day after attacking and occupying Denmark and Norway: *"…it only aims at preventing Scandinavia from becoming a battlefield for the British to extend the war…. Germany does not conduct a war against small nations."* This was followed by

11

a five-year military occupation of Denmark and Norway.

- Jan. 30, 1942, Hitler speech in Berlin: *"My fame… will consist in… works of peace."* [8]

Trump:

Most politicians, at some point, may stretch the truth or even resort to outright lies to navigate challenging situations. Donald Trump is no exception. However, a notable distinction exists: for Trump, lying appears to be the rule rather than the exception—and this pattern has been well-documented. (Refer to the special section for more details.) While Hitler manipulated the truth shrewdly and cunningly, particularly on political issues, Trump escalated the practice of lying to a new level, using deceit as a standard tool. In August 2020, the Senior White House Correspondent for the Huffington Post directly addressed this during a press conference, asking Trump, *"Mr. President, after three and a half years, do you regret all the lies, all the dishonesties you have told the American people?"* Trump's response was to deflect, pointing to another journalist and saying, *"Next question, please."*

He later remarked in a CNN interview: *"When covering someone like Donald Trump, who is prone to lying, it becomes futile to inquire about issues like taxes or the COVID vaccine because if he doesn't know the answer, he fabricates one. The pressing question we all have is: why does he do this? We deserve an answer. We are in a democracy; that's why we have debates. But it's not acceptable to eschew the truth."*

Furthermore, Trump's untruths often concerned matters easily debunked, such as claiming that the COVID virus *"was totally under control"* and *"was disappearing."* Coupled with his dismissal of preventive vaccinations, he implied to Americans that there was little need for concern. Yet, America was among the countries hardest hit by the COVID-19 virus.

Another example: In his 2020 campaign, he repeatedly claimed that he was once named Michigan's Man of the Year. He wasn't.[9]

The list of Trump's falsehoods is extensive, with additional examples highlighted in the subsequent section.

4. Make our country great again. "Germany—only for Germans." Nationalism. Patriotism.

Hitler:

- **Slogan and Propaganda:**

In prison, Adolf Hitler, assisted by Rudolf Hess, penned his political ideas in *"Mein Kampf"* (My Struggle), published in 1925. Upon his release, Hitler and his allies vigorously campaigned under the banner of these concepts. The central slogan, *"Make Germany Great Again,"* resonated particularly with the lower middle class and the unemployed, rooted in the notion that Germany needed to reclaim its pre-WWI *"natural greatness."* Hitler frequently proclaimed, *"Politicians are corrupt,"* and decried that the

German people had been *"stabbed in the back,"* instilling a strong sense of nationalism as a foundational principle.

- **Big Lie—Antisemitism as Strategy:**

Hitler and his Nazi Party allies advanced the claim that for Germany to achieve its supposed destined greatness, it had to purge Jews from society. They propagated the extreme antisemitic message, ***"Germany—only for Germans,"*** to garner support for this egregious stance. Despite the difficulty of convincing the populace—given the Jews' integration and generally positive relations within German society—the Nazis persisted with a relentless spread of lies, branding Jews as significant contributors to economic decline and dubbing them ***"vermin."*** This insidious campaign gradually swayed public opinion, paving the way for the horrific genocide that followed, with millions of Jews being exterminated in concentration camps.

- **Targeting Socialists, and Communists, and political opponents:**

Identifying additional scapegoats, the Nazi Party targeted Socialists and Communists as enemies of the state, initiating a brutal crackdown that began in the early 1930s and led to the assassination of many of their leaders.

Through cunning party leadership, heavy promotion of lies, and helped by the great depression from 1929 to 1932, Hitler took power in 1933. The rest is tragic history. [10]

Trump:

- ## Slogans and propaganda.

Donald Trump, with his infamous slogan *"**Make America Great Again,**"* managed to capture the attention of a broad swath of the American population, using heavy promotion and demagogic tactics similar to those employed by Hitler. Hitler leveraged the economic depression and the Big Lie about Jews to stoke nationalism and garner support. Trump's slogan tapped into a growing sense of despair and hopelessness within the U.S., serving as a rallying cry for his supporters.

Trump's unfiltered and abrasive language marked a stark departure from typical political discourse, which enchanted many voters. He frequently labeled his political opponents as *"useless,"* *"lazy,"* and *"corrupt."* He vowed *to "drain the Washington D.C. swamp,"* positioning himself as a relatable *"man of the people"* despite his wealth and elite status. His nationalistic stance was evident throughout his presidency from 2016 to 2020, during which he abandoned several international agreements and even threatened to withdraw from NATO.

- ## The Big Lie—Allegations of a *"Rigged Election"*:

Echoing Hitler's strategy, Trump responded to his 2020 election defeat with his version of the Big Lie, claiming the election was *"stolen."* This assertion resonated deeply, rapidly consolidating a cult-like following among his existing MAGA supporters. The term *"patriotism"* began to circulate uncritically among his base, mirroring the gradual escalation of rhetoric and actions that characterized Hitler's followers.

- **Targeting Minorities and Political Opponents:**

Drawing disturbing parallels with Hitler's language, Trump has used similarly dehumanizing rhetoric to describe Muslims, communists, and illegal immigrants, employing terms like *"vermin"* and accusing them of *"sucking the blood of American people."* His focus on strengthening U.S. borders and demanding more from international agreements underscore his nationalistic agenda. Coupled with his endorsement from groups espousing white supremacist ideologies, and his scapegoating of socialists and communists, Trump's rhetoric and policies paint the picture of a nationalist in the most pejorative sense of the word.

5. Personality:

Could the striking similarities between Trump and Hitler be linked to their personalities?

Hitler:

Hitler is believed to have had Asperger's syndrome, which manifested in obsessions with conspiracy theories and an intolerance for dissent. He was often viewed as desperate for recognition of his supposed genius. Frequently described as an egomaniac who *"only loved himself,"* Hitler was a textbook narcissist with a flair for self-dramatization. He was sometimes called a *"self-obsessed clown"* noted for his erratic, impulsive behavior. A recent German biographer, reflecting on Hitler's life, noted his *"characteristic fondness for superlatives."*[11]

Trump:

Donald Trump shares several of these traits with Hitler. Like Hitler, Trump is a narcissist who embraces conspiracy theories and shows little tolerance for those who challenge him, constantly seeking admiration to bolster his grandiose self-image.

Undoubtedly, these observations suggest that both figures could be considered *"two of a kind,"* exhibiting similar personality traits or, perhaps, disorders.

6. Great demagogues:[12]

"To be recognized as a demagogue, a politician must fulfill four criteria:

- *Be a "man of the masses," a distinction typically earned through attacking elites.*
- *Have the ability to evoke intense passion.*
- *Utilize that passion for political advantage.*
- *Test and violate established laws and accepted norms if it serves their agenda.*

This approach allows the demagogue to forge a state within a state—a vast cult—that pledges allegiance solely to him.[13]

Criteria Easily Met by Both Men:

Hitler:

From early on, Hitler demonstrated his talent as a mesmerizing public speaker, capable of swaying the masses. For instance, at his first political meetings in Munich, the crowd enthusiastically cheered him for demanding a new German order to replace what he claimed was incompetent and inefficient democratic leadership.

"Hitler adapted the content of his speeches to suit the tastes of his lower-middle-class, nationalist-conservative, ethnic-chauvinist, and anti-Semitic listeners," writes Mr. Ullrich in his biography of Hitler.[14] *"He peppered his speeches with coarse phrases and put-downs of hecklers, promising to lead Germany to a new era of national greatness,"* though he was typically vague about his actual plan.

Ullrich also noted, after having read Hitler's speeches: *"It seems amazing that he attracted larger and larger audiences with repeated mantralike phrases consisting largely of accusations, vows of revenge, and promises for the future."* Hitler leaned on two primary principles when he spoke:

The understanding of the masses is feeble; effective propaganda needs to be boiled down to a few slogans persistently repeated until the very last individual has come to grasp the idea that has been put forward.

Propaganda must appeal to the emotions—not the reasoning powers—of the crowd.

Using and applying this understanding as a tactic proved highly successful for Hitler, but it led to disastrous consequences in world history.

Trump:

Trump, like Hitler, is a great demagogue. However, experts who have compared his speeches with Hitler's are unanimous in their opinion that Hitler was far more eloquent, deliberate, and knowledgeable. In contrast, Trump is more impulsive, less articulate, and more straightforward. Michael Singer:[15]

"Trump has managed to portray himself as an outsider of the established system who can be a champion for the average Joe and Jane. He has fed off the discontent many Americans feel towards politics. His willingness to brashly call out leaders has made many people who have felt overlooked by their leaders feel acknowledged for the first time. The connection many feel with him is so strong that it has blinded them to the more dangerous side of Trump."

No doubt, Hitler and Trump were both mesmerizing public speakers, extremely good at stirring people's emotions in their directions, and, unfortunately, cunning demagogues.

Result: *"Donald Trump was the first demagogue to be elected President of the United States."*

7. Harassing, hateful, and threatening language.

Hitler:

Hitler used language to dehumanize, delegitimize, and intimidate his perceived enemies. Jews, communists, and socialists became his prime targets. As early as 1920, in his political autobiography, *"Mein Kampf"* (My Struggle), Hitler employed inflammatory language. He described communism as *"Judaism"* and Jews as *"vermin (parasites)."* This dangerous rhetoric became a recurring theme throughout the 1930s, leading to the persecution of Jews, other non-Aryan races, and eventually communists and socialists. The day after he was appointed Chancellor of Germany in 1933, he wrote: *"The Jews, like vermin, form a line from Potsdamer Platz until Anhalter Bahnhof… The only way to smoke out the vermin is to expel them."*

Trump:

Trump's mocking style from his presidential period has become darker after the 2020 election loss. Like Hitler, he has started using language to dehumanize, delegitimize, and intimidate his perceived enemies. He has begun to use Mafia-like indirect threats and, in many cases, described individuals who cross his interests so negatively that his MAGA followers have been inspired to react with direct threats and actions against those persons. Trump's prime targets are illegal immigrants, minorities, and anyone who opposes him, whether legally or politically. He publicly stated in November 2023 (on Veterans Day) that *"we will root out the communists, Marxists, fascists, and the radical left thugs that live like vermin within the confines of our country that lie and steal and cheat on elections."* He has also said that *"immigrants are poisoning the blood of our country."*

His threats have become numerous, appearing in campaign rallies or on *"Truth Social,"* his social media platform. Here are a couple of examples illustrating how dangerous Trump's language has become:

In September 2023, he said of General Milley, former Head of the Joint Chiefs of Staff, that *"Mark Milley's phone call to reassure China in the aftermath of the storming of the Capitol on January 6, 2021, was an act so egregious that, in times gone by, the punishment would have been DEATH."* As a result, Milley has received death threats and had to take special protective measures for himself and his family.

In November 2023, after a court arraignment, he stated, *"If you go after me, I am coming after you."*

Is this language worthy of a future president? Instead, it seems more like the language of a Mafia boss and Hitler. How did the Congressional representatives react? Silence. Thus, they were passively but undeniably paving the way for a growing general acceptance of a new norm of hateful language.

8. Blaming others.

Hitler:

Hitler blamed the communists for setting fire to the Reichstag (Congress). He attributed the catastrophic

German economy after WWI to Jews, labeling them as an inferior race who stole jobs from *"pure"* Germans. He even blamed his teachers for his poor grades, remarking, *"In school, I had bad marks in German. That idiot of a teacher spoiled the German language for me."*

Trump:

Similarly, Trump has a history of blaming everyone and everything for problems while taking credit for success, regardless of his involvement. He succinctly expressed this attitude in a November 2022 interview with News Nation, commenting on the upcoming midterm elections: *"If they win, I should get all the credit; if they lose, I should not be blamed at all."*[16] Before and after that, he has blamed WHO and former administrations for late action on the COVID-19 virus. He frequently targets the *"fake media,"* asserting, *"… much of the anger in society is caused by the purposely false and inaccurate reporting of the mainstream media."* This prompted John Brennan, former CIA head, to retort: *"Look in the mirror. Your inflammatory rhetoric, insults, lies, and encouragement of physical violence are disgraceful."*

9. Racism.

Hitler:

Racism was a fundamental element of Nazism. Hitler's views on inequality extended not only to races but also to nations and individuals. In *"Mein Kampf,"* he depicted Jews as *"destroyers of culture,"* *"a parasite within the nation,"* and *"a menace."* He considered the *"Aryan Race" to be superior—an idea akin to the notion of "White supremacy."* In 1934, Hitler declared:

"If I can send the flowers of the German nation into the hell of war without pity, then surely I have the right to remove millions of an inferior race that breeds like vermin." (This was a reference to the Jews.)

Hitler repeatedly described Jews as *"poisoning the blood-stream of our country."*

Trump:

Racism has always been evident in both Trump's private attitude and his political agenda. Despite his repeated claims of being *"the least racist person,"* reality suggests otherwise. Recent statements in 2023 and 2024 have made this abundantly clear: *"Undocumented immigrants are poisoning the blood of our country."* This statement openly supports the *"white replacement theory,"* which believes that the government is intentionally replacing white citizens with nonwhite individuals.

Let me repeat his statement at a rally on Veteran's Day in mid-November 2023, *"We pledge to you that we will root out the communists, the Marxists, fascists, and the radical left thugs that live like vermin within the confines of our country.'"*

Regrettably, and perhaps unsurprisingly, GOP leaders are now, knowingly or unknowingly, embracing what can be described as a Hitler/Goebbels–like racist agenda. As Ari Gelber stated on MSNBC on December 3, 2021, *"Trump is substituting Jews with Muslims and other non-whites… The Nazi state exploited such racial distinctions as part of their discriminatory and coercive policies, which ultimately led to the Holocaust."*

Trump's history of racism predates his presidency:

In the 1970's (!), the US Department of Justice sued him for racial discrimination (for refusing to rent to black persons).[17]

In the 1980s at Trump's Castle, Kip Brown, one of the employees, remembers: *"When Donald and Ivana came to the casino, the bosses would order all the black people off the floor."*[18]

In 1989, Trump criticized John O'Donnell, former president of Trump Plaza Hotel and Casino in Atlantic City, for employing a Black accountant, remarking: *"I think that the guy is lazy. And it's probably not his fault because laziness is a trait in blacks. It's not anything they can control."*

Following Barack Obama's election as the first Black President of the U.S., Trump falsely claimed that Obama was not born in the U.S. He also insinuated that Obama might not have been a sufficiently good student to gain admission to Columbia or Harvard Law School, commenting, *"I heard he was a terrible student. Terrible."* (On the contrary, former president Barack Obama graduated with magna cum laude in 1991 from Harvard. Professor Laurence Tribe has called him *"the most impressive student I have ever taught."*)

These and the following examples reveal a consistent pattern in Trump's conduct and comments regarding people of color, among numerous other instances:

- While campaigning in 2015, Trump referred to Mexican immigrants as criminals and rapists and proposed banning all Muslims from entering the US.

- He criticized NFL players who silently protested systemic racism in America by kneeling during the national anthem.

- When discussing immigrants from Haiti and African countries, he asked, *"Why are we having all these people from shithole countries come here?"* He then suggested that the US should instead welcome more immigrants from countries like Norway. As a Norwegian, I might be expected to take pride in such a distinction, but I do not. The measure of good and evil in people depends not on their race but on the economic and cultural conditions that have evolved in their local environments.

- In one of his many racially charged tweets, he claimed that Black and Brown members of Congress—Pressley, Omar, Ocasio-Cortez, and Tlaib—originated from *"countries whose govern-ments are a complete and total catastrophe"* and suggested that they should *"go back"* to these coun-tries. Such statements are unabashedly racist.

10. Tax evasion.

Hitler:

After rising to power, Hitler avoided taxes on his income and allowances. In 1934, one year after becoming Chancellor, the Munich tax office fined him for failing to declare his income or file tax returns. He responded by ordering a state secretary of the Ministry of Finance to intervene—resulting in a declaration from the head of the Munich tax office, *"all tax reports delivering substance for a tax obligation by the Führer are annulled from the start. The Führer is therefore tax-exempt."* [19]And that was the end of Hitler paying any taxes.

Trump:

As is well known to most Americans and many world-wide, Mr. Trump has utilized every conceivable loop-hole—and an army of lawyers—to minimize his taxes. Although he hasn't yet achieved Hitler's level of personal tax exemption, it's clear he has not hesitated to attempt leveraging federal executive departments to his benefit while in power.

Some of his tax avoidance strategies may fall within legal gray areas, while others push the limits of the law extensively. It is challenging to fully assess these actions, as Trump has persistently refused to release his tax return documents, leaving us to speculate about his reasons.

Nevertheless, The New York Times obtained his tax records, revealing that Trump paid no net federal income tax for most of the previous 15 years. It also disclosed that many of these tax evasions were linked to fraudulent practices, resulting in substantial penalties.

11. Contempt for the law.

Hitler:

Upon seizing power, Hitler quickly banned or suppressed the independent press and orchestrated the burning of books he deemed *"un-German."*

By March 1933, Hitler had made it clear that his government would do away with all norms of separation of powers and the rule of law.[20]

He undermined the independent judiciary by harassing and dismissing judges who held socialist views or other perspectives that conflicted with the Nazi Party's agenda.

"The German nation, under the leadership of Hitler, destroyed the respect for the law, ...the recognition of legality as the decisive motive of action or forbearance in domestic as well as foreign relations."[21]

Notably, Hitler harbored a strong disdain for judges because the pursuit of justice often obstructed his methods. Addressing the judiciary in a speech in the Reichstag on April 26, 1942, Hitler said, *"...From now on, I shall intervene in these cases and remove from office those judges who evidently do not understand the demand of the hour."*[22]

According to the US military tribunal in Nuremberg, *"This menacing declaration by the Fuhrer eradicated the last vestiges of judicial independence in Germany."*

Trump:

Similar to Hitler, the judiciary appears to pose significant obstacles to Trump's disregard for the law, both before, during, and after his presidency. Trump seems to believe that, as a former president, he is above the law and a target of corrupt prosecutors and judges. Consequently, he has increasingly demonstrated contempt for the law, openly demeaning and insulting anyone in the legal profession who stands in his way—district attorneys, judges, prosecutors, court staff, and witnesses alike. No one, and nothing appears sacred to Trump anymore.

Statements such as *"The FBI and the Justice Department have become vicious monsters…"* (from a speech in Pennsylvania on September 3, 2022) and accusations of corruption directed at judges illustrate Trump's consistent attacks on legal representatives and judicial institutions. Trump is now, with the authority of being a former American president and a current Republican Party leader, on a path to undermine the whole judiciary system through such statements.[23] The same way Hitler did on his way to make the judiciary a tool *"to understand the demand of the hour."*

12. Pardoning criminals, not for injustice done, but for having helped the pardoner.

Hitler:

Hitler pardoned SS guards in the Dachau concentration camp after they were found guilty of mistreating prisoners and given prison sentences. That put a practical and definitive end to legal proceedings in regular courts against operations in the camps.[24] However, after WWII ended, an international tribunal managed to bring some of these individuals to trial, often resulting in severe judgments, including against Hitler's closest collaborators.

Trump:

In the U.S., Presidential pardons have become a regular practice ever since George Washington granted the first high-profile federal pardon in 1795 to leaders of the Whiskey Rebellion on his final day in office.[25] It is not unique to Trump. However, in Trump's case, while technically within the bounds of legality, most of his pardons were not issued due to perceived injustices done to the convicted. Instead, they benefited individuals who had somehow served Trump's political or economic interests, such as Steve Bannon, Roger Stone, Paul Manafort, George Papadopoulos, and many others.

13. Support from business magnates and smaller donors—and skillfully channeling funds into their private projects.

Hitler:

In the 1920s, the Nazi Party had limited representation in Congress but developed the most robust financial base among political parties, mainly due to support from the business sector. Wealthy benefactors, both domestic and international, provided significant donations. Notable contributors included The Bechsteins, owners of a piano manufacturing factory, the Thyssen steel company, and the

Krupp corporation. Some Americans also supported the party until the attack on Pearl Harbor in 1941. General Motors and Ford conducted substantial business with Nazi Germany, supplying vehicles to the Nazi army. Henry Ford was a well-known antisemite, and Ford's German branch handed Hitler 35,000 Reichsmarks in April 1939 as a birthday gift—all of this with full acceptance of their American headquarters.[26]

Unsurprisingly, Hitler adeptly diverted much of the party's income from donations into personal ventures, including his private residences like the Berghof and the Eagle's Nest. He also utilized *"slush funds,"* comprised of contributions from various benefactors, to cover his personal expenses. Economic journalist Wolfgang Zdral remarked, *"He drove a Mercedes, which was incredibly expensive at the time, could afford extensive travels, and had sufficient funds to finance his propaganda efforts."*

Trump:

Here, too, a striking similarity emerges between him and Hitler. Trump has privately received financing from wealthy business owners (the Murdoch family, Koch brothers, Rebekah and Robert Mercer, among others.) The two biggest industries that supported his 2020 campaign were the casino/gambling industry ($47 million) and real estate companies (nearly $40 million).[27]

The oil and gas industry has also made substantial donations to his candidacy in both the 2020 campaign and the upcoming 2024 election.

Additionally, *"ordinary"* people, primarily from his MAGA base, continue to contribute to Trump's current campaign funds. Unfortunately, much of this funding does not go towards his campaign. It is diverted to cover his legal fees through *"slush funds"* like *"Trump Victory"* and the *"Trump Make America Great Again Committee,"* among other special arrangements. In 2020 alone, over $7 million was estimated to have been funneled into Trump's private business.

According to documents from the Federal Election Commission, Trump's political action committees spent the majority of their received funds on his legal expenses, which exceeded a staggering $50 million in 2023. Trump faces 91 felony counts across four criminal cases and civil charges. As of now, he has lost two civil cases, including the E. Carroll defamation case, where the jury ordered him to pay an $83 million fee.

14. Criminal entourage.

Hitler:

Hitler's inner circle and entourage, with a few exceptions, became accomplices in his criminal regime. After Hitler consolidated sole power through the Enabling Act in 1933, he systematically sidelined political opponents. He established his cadre of loyal collaborators, forming an evil and virtually omnipotent cabinet comprising over 25 individuals. Most of these individuals were educated and reasonably intelligent figures such as Goebbels, Himmler, Göring, Bormann, Frick, Keitel, Hess, Speer, and others.

Without their support, Hitler would never have succeeded in his ambitions. However, they were quickly consumed by the vast power bestowed upon them and lost their moral bearings.

These persons, with a few exceptions, contributed to grave crimes in the decade to come, for which they were severely punished right after the war.[28] [29]

Trump:

Many of Trump's current and former inner circle are already entangled in legal conflicts.

The resemblance between Hitler's appointees and Trump's entourage is striking. Figures like Bannon, Flynn, Spicer, McCarthy, McConnell, and others have been influential and appear poised to support him if he succeeds. (The two last ones are not his inner circle and are not involved in any criminalities, but were instrumental in keeping Trump's grip on the Party leadership by blocking any attempts to hold Trump accountable for his actions in trying to overturn the 2020 election.) [30]

Most of Trump's loyal circle is well-known; some have been dismissed or sidelined (e.g., Powell, Giuliani, Eastman, Lindell, among others), while others operate more discreetly under the radar. Newcomers may also be drawn by the allure of power should Trump succeed. Here is a rough overview based on current information (in alphabetical order):

- **Steve Bannon, Trump Campaign CEO, and Senior White House Advisor:**

Steve Bannon is a highly influential figure who has played a pivotal role in Trump's strategies. His demeanor and intellect draw comparisons to Hitler's propagandist, Goebbels.

In August 2020, Bannon was charged with fraud and money laundering. He allegedly enriched himself and two associates through a scheme called *"We Build the Wall,"* which misappropriated millions of dollars in donations from Trump supporters. Trump pardoned him before the trial.

Two years later, in July 2022, Bannon was found guilty of criminal contempt of Congress for refusing to comply with a subpoena from the congressional committee investigating the events of January 6. He was sentenced to four months in prison but has appealed.

- **Elliot Broidy, Former RNC Finance Chairman and Republican Mega-Donor:**

Elliot Broidy pleaded guilty to one count of conspiracy to violate the Foreign Agents Registration Act (2020) for his unregistered lobbying work on behalf of a foreign country. He resigned from his RNC Chairmanship after it was revealed that he had paid $1.6 million in hush money to a former Playboy model to conceal their affair. Notably, Trump's then-lawyer, Michael Cohen, was involved in arranging this deal.

- **Michael Cohen, former Trump legal advisor:**

Michael Cohen, pressured by Trump to commit fraud on his behalf, stands out as one of the few who have broken free from Trump's influence. Cohen has publicly cautioned others about Trump's disregard for the law and the threat to U.S. democracy if he were to be elected for a second term. His inclusion here underscores the legal risks of being part of Trump's inner circle.

- **Mike Flynn, former Trump security adviser**:

Pleaded guilty to lying to the FBI about communications with Russian officials. Trump pardoned him before being convicted.[31]

- **Rick Gates, Trump's Deputy Campaign Manager, and Mana Fort's Close Ally:**

Rick Gates pleaded guilty to conspiracy and lying to the FBI concerning the Mueller investigation. He admitted to assisting Manafort in laundering Ukrainian money and was sentenced to 45 days in prison plus three years of probation.

- **Rudy Giuliani, Trump's former legal advisor:**

Rudy Giuliani is facing a criminal investigation in Georgia led by Fulton County's District Attorney for his role in attempting to overturn the election results in that state. Court hearings are scheduled for later in 2024. In another case, Giuliani was found guilty of defamation against two poll workers in Georgia who subsequently received death threats. He has filed an appeal.

- **Mike Lindell, an extremely loud vocal supporter of Donald Trump's election fraud claims:**

Mike Lindell alleged that voting machines were manipulated to *"steal"* the 2020 election. Despite claiming to have proof, Lindell failed to substantiate his allegations. In February 2024, he was fined $5 million for defamation against a software engineer who challenged Lindell's assertions about China's interference in the 2020 U.S. presidential election. Lindell has announced plans to appeal the decision, asserting that the engineer is undeserving of compensation. Time will tell whether his appeal is successful. Lindell is among many Trump supporters who have made bold assertions about the 2020 election without providing credible evidence.

- **Paul Manafort, Former Trump 2016 Campaign Manager:**

Paul Manafort has a controversial background. He previously worked as an advocate for arms dealer Abdul Rahman Al Assir, associated with dictator Marcos, and assisted Viktor Yanukovych in becoming Ukraine's leader under Russian influence. He was thrown out of Ukraine in the revolution after Russia had *"annexed"* by military force the Crimea part of Ukraine.[32]

On September 14, 2016, Manafort pleaded guilty to conspiracy charges related to money earned from working as an unregistered foreign agent for Ukraine. Later, Trump pardoned him. In April 2022, federal authorities claimed $3 million from hidden offshore accounts. The case remains open.

- **Peter Navarro, a Trump White House advisor**:

Peter Navarro was indicted for criminal contempt of Congress for failing to respond to a subpoena from the congressional committee investigating January 6. He was sentenced to three months in jail.

- **George Papadopoulos, member of Trump's 2016 campaign policy team:**

George Papadopoulos, pleaded guilty, like Mike Flynn, to lying to the FBI about contacts with Russians. Trump later pardoned him.

- **Roger Stone, a long-time friend, associate, and advisor to Trump:**

Roger Stone, claimed he convinced Trump to run for president. In November 2019, he was convicted of seven criminal counts, including lying under oath to lawmakers investigating Russian interference in the 2016 U.S. election, lying to Congress, and witness tampering. Stone was sentenced to 3 years in prison but pardoned by Trump just before beginning his sentence.

- **Alan Weisselberg, former chief financial officer for the Trump Organization:**

Alan Weisselberg pleaded guilty in August 2022 to 15 counts of criminal conduct, including engineering tax fraud. He was initially sentenced to 3 months in jail but was released after serving half his sentence. The Trump Organization expressed support for Weisselberg, describing him as a *"fine and honorable man"* who had been *"harassed, persecuted, and threatened by law enforcement."* Months later, after serving his first jail sentence, Weisselberg was indicted for lying under oath and had to serve an additional three months.

15. Failed attempts to seize power illegally.

Hitler:

The National Socialist movement, led by Hitler and his party, the Nationalsozialistische Deutsche Arbeiterpartei (soon better known as the Nazi Party), attempted to overthrow parliamentary democracy through a failed coup d'état in Munich in November 1923. Hitler, already a skilled demagogue, incited the masses to march to Berlin with the rallying cry: *"Morning will either find us with a national government in Germany or find us dead."*

However, the regular army swiftly crushed the rebellion, and the coup failed. Hitler, Rudolf Hess, and Hermann Göring, among other leaders, were arrested and subsequently sentenced to jail two weeks later. Half a year later, Hitler and other leaders of the failed coup d'état were found guilty of treason. Hitler was sentenced to 5 years in prison—but was released after 13 months. [33]

Trump:

Ninety-seven years after Hitler's failed coup d'état in 1923, Trump replicated Hitler's maneuver almost exactly by inciting an attack on the Capitol to seize power illegally. Trump not only had a hand in the planning but was deeply involved in the execution of the January 6th attempt to overturn a legitimate presidential election. Addressing the crowd just before the attack, Trump echoed Hitler's sentiment, stating, *"We fight like hell. And if you don't fight like hell, you won't have a country."*

Similar to Hitler, Trump ultimately failed, and hundreds of his MAGA followers have been sentenced to prison terms, some as long as 15 years. He currently faces two criminal trials for his active role, likely to take place in 2024. However, legal proceedings are moving slower than a hundred years ago; only time will reveal the outcome.

16. Supporter violence against targeted victims.

Hitler and the SA:

Hitler and the Nazi Party established their militia in 1922 to safeguard party meetings and act as the party's army. Most of its members were lower-middle-class Germans left unemployed due to Germany's dire economic situation after World War I. They wore uniforms called *"Sturm Abteilung"* (Storm Troopers) and were brainwashed to believe they could restore Germany's greatness, viewing communists and Jews as obstacles. They quickly gained a reputation as *"brown shirts,"* harassing political adversaries and engaging in street violence. Their actions escalated after the Nazi Party's electoral success in 1930, becoming Hitler's militant arm with brutal antisemitic and anti-democratic activities, including forcibly abducting and eliminating opponents.

Starting with a few thousand members in 1922, the SA grew into a massive army of four million soldiers. In 1933, following Hitler's rise to power, the SA was incorporated as an official government organization. They merged with the regular police force and were granted *"carte blanche"* to arrest and torture not only political opponents but personal enemies as well. By 1934, they had become such a strong force that Hitler feared their leaders would rebel against him in a military coup, and on Hitler's demand, their leaders were killed. Executed by the SS death squadron, the now most feared part of the Nazi Party. The SA's power was reduced but continued to exist.[34]

Trump and the MAGA Cult:

With his infamous *"Make America Great Again"* (MAGA) slogan—copied from Reagan but trademarked by Trump—he has managed, much like Hitler, to appeal to a sizable segment of the American population who believe the U.S. urgently needs to reclaim its status and identity from *"threatening forces."* Unlike the homogenous group of mainly lower-middle-class unemployed workers that formed the Nazi militia, Trump's MAGA supporters are a more diverse group, including significant representation from the middle class and college-educated individuals. Trump does not need to organize them into military units as Hitler did; with the internet and social media at his disposal, he can mobilize thousands in an instant to act violently against his perceived *"enemies."*

"Right now, these people (MAGA supporters) feel like they're losing their country and their identity. They feel like they're being displaced by communities of color, by feminists, and by immigrants. They are motivated by what they see as an existential threat to their way of life," said Christopher S. Parker, co-author of a recent research on MAGA supporters.[35]

As early as 2015, a nationwide poll showed that MAGA supporters believed in an authoritarian-style government. MacWilliams, who conducted the study, stated, *"Authoritarians obey. They rally to and follow strong leaders. And they respond aggressively to outsiders, especially when they feel threatened."* He boldly claimed, *"One Weird Trait That Predicts Whether You're a Trump Supporter. And it's not gender, age, income, race or religion. It's authoritarianism."* As we have seen during 2023 and 2024, with more and more of Trump's fans encouraged by his authoritarian style, I think we have to give MacWilliams the right.

The January 6 attack on Congress fully demonstrated the willingness of Trump supporters to follow the signals from their authoritarian leader, Donald Trump, by using violence instead of democracy. It didn't stop there. Hundreds of election workers across the U.S. were threatened—Not by walking from door to door as did Hitler's

"Brownshirts," but via phone terror, the internet, letters, some with death threats.[36]

Constantly inflamed by Trump, MAGA supporters have engaged in physical and verbal attacks against any representative of the law or anyone who seems to obstruct Trump's agenda. In 2024, these actions have escalated rather than decreased, in line with the signals given by their leader, Donald Trump.

The step from here to more violence seems short. Who could stop this? Donald Trump. Who can and wants to escalate this? Donald Trump. No matter how we look at it, dangers lie ahead. Trump controls the MAGA supporters much like Hitler created and controlled the Brownshirts.

And it doesn't look good. Since his 2020 election loss, Donald Trump has shown increasing signs of an authoritarian leadership style. In 2023, he even hinted that, if elected President in 2024, he wants to be a *"dictator on the first day."* A joke or a wish? His supporters are indeed applauding. The question is: How many? Will this extreme leadership style scare his supporters or attract them? The 2024 election will provide the answer.

The similarities between Adolf Hitler and Donald Trump are a stark warning of Trump's possible negative impact on America and world politics in the coming decades. As we will see later, warnings about Trump have increased in number and intensity parallel to his increasingly narcissistic behavior.

CHAPTER 2

TRUMP'S EARLY YEARS AND HOW IT AFFECTED HIS PERSONALITY

D onald Trump grew up with a mother prone to severe illness and a dominant, abusive father. Various sources close to Trump's family during those years suggest that his father had a powerful influence on Donald's personality.

According to Donald's niece, Mary Trump, a psychologist, his father largely ignored him during his early years. When Donald was three, his mother became very ill and had to abandon him. From early on until his teens, the only attention he received from his father was through yelling, criticism, or punishment. He also witnessed his father verbally abusing his older brother and saw his parents' emotionally abusive marriage. This had a decisive impact on Donald's personality. As Mary Trump put it: *"Too much"* (abusiveness and repression from his father from early childhood) and *"not enough"* of feeling safe and loved. *"Donald suffered deprivations that would scar him for life."*

"To be able to cope," she writes: *"Donald began to develop powerful but primitive defenses, marked by increasing hostility to others and a seeming indifference to his mother's absence and father's neglect....In place of his emotional needs grew a kind of grievance and behaviors—including bullying, disrespect, and aggressiveness—that served their purpose in the moment but became more problematic over time. With appropriate care and attention, these traumas might have been overcome."* [37]

D'Antonio, a later biographer of Trump, describes a similar pattern. Donald's father was so busy *"scheming and manipulating"* his business that Donald soon became an uncontrolled bully. Despite living in a posh, mansion-like building and being materially spoiled, he completely lacked the parental love any child unconsciously craves. Mary Trump described him as becoming an *"asshole"* during this period.

A seemingly grave knife incident prompted his father to send him away to the New York Military Academy to prevent further trouble and instill discipline. (Donald and a friend were caught showing knives in the subway, but according to Gwenda Blair, a Trump biographer, they "had nothing bad in mind, only wanted to look cool.") Donald was 13 years old at the time. Mary Trump noted that *"Up till then, Donald Trump had practically no positive childhood experiences that could buffer the abuse he endured. Unfortunately, for Donald and everybody else on this planet, those behaviors hardened into personality traits."*

Donald's *"anonymous"* educational years.

Starting with his years at New York Military Academy, followed by his four years at Fordham University and Wharton Business School, Donald's personality seemed to deviate from the narcissistic pattern he was almost destined for. At NYMA, he adapted quickly, according to his fellow cadets and officers. He was well-liked, eventually rising to the rank of company captain. At Fordham and Wharton, he went relatively unnoticed.

During these nine years, from 1959 to 1968, being away from his family, the influence on him by his father was sporadic, almost non-existent. There was little or nothing to trigger Donald's latent narcissism. He escaped being drafted to military service using college and medical *("bone spurs")* deferments.[38]

After graduating from university, he joined his father's business. It was well-known that his father had ties with the Mafia and often used methods that were—to say it mildly—not 100% ethical.[39] Donald soon learned the *"tricks of the trade,"* many of them on the shady side, both ethically and economically. Parallel with this, his father's influence was re-established; this time, his father's abusiveness was replaced with installing in Donald the importance of being *"tough,"* a *"killer,"* and *"the king."* Inclusive deals with the mafia. *"Trump's business dealings with the mob or mob-related characters are widely documented."* [40]

*"Life is mainly combat; the law of the jungle rules; pretty much all that matters is winning or losing, **and rules are made to be broken.**"*[41]

CHAPTER 3

TRUMP'S RISE TO POWER. FROM BUSINESSMAN AND TV PERSONALITY TO PRESIDENT

His business career.

Let's begin with Donald Trump's claims:

- *"My father gave me a 'small loan' of $1 million to get started."*
- *"I borrowed 1 million dollars and built it into a company worth more than $10 billion!"*
- *"I am a self-made billionaire."*
- *"People writing books saying I got this and that, that I got a lot of money—I got peanuts!"*
- *"My father did not leave a great fortune."*
- *"I built this empire, and I did it by myself. And if I can do that, look what I can do for the country."*

Well, not the truth.

After an extensive investigation by a team from The New York Times (three journalists over 18 months), they published an article stating that *"before Donald had turned 30, he had received close to $9 million from his father. Over the longer haul, he received upward of what, in today's dollars, would be $413 million."* He continues to receive recurrent income from lease payments arranged by his father, such as those from Starrett City. He was almost a millionaire from the age of 3, receiving the equivalent of a doctor's salary by lease payments originating from the Beach Haven complex in N.Y. [42]

His grandfather and father laid the foundation.

The career in real estate started with Donald Trump's grandfather, Friedrich Trump (1869-1918). Friedrich entered real estate during the Klondike Gold Rush, operating a bar, restaurant, and brothel in Northern British Columbia, which made him a small fortune. He then moved to New York, where he laid the foundation for the family's real estate business. (The family's original name was Drumpf, and Fred even spoke German, but they tried to conceal this, partly because it wasn't advantageous to be German in America just after WWII.)

His son and Donald Trump's father, Fred Trump (1905–1999), went into construction and building, seizing many opportunities during the 1920s building boom. He held many buildings, mainly in Queens, at the start of the Depression in 1929. Maybe with some help, he could use *"government subsidies and loopholes"* from his connections with the mafia and his cynical methods to get business deals through. [43]

Upon his death, his family estimated Fred Trump's estate to be $250 million to $300 million, though he had "only" $1.9 million in cash.

Donald's *"flying business start"*—founded on his father's wealth.

Now, thanks to hundreds of millions of dollars in accumulated capital from his father, most of it in real estate, Donald Trump had a solid foundation for his business. Because Trump never revealed his tax returns (being the first American president to refuse), it is difficult to estimate the actual values of the Trump Corporation. It is likely more than the $413 million the New York Times estimated he had received by the beginning of this century and less than the *"more than $10 billion"* he claimed in 2022.

Forbes has made a year-to-year analysis, estimating the value to be 1.7 billion dollars in 2000 (what he and his father did together) and increasing to 2.6 billion dollars in 2023.[44] This represents a good doubling if these estimates are accurate. Who wouldn't be happy with those numbers?

But there are two problems with these numbers:

- The numbers are uncertain because the Trump family does not wish to reveal them. They could be higher or lower, but there are strong indications that the portfolio contains overvalued assets. Also, the debt amounts are unknown, an essential part of the equation.

- Extensive tax evasion schemes might have contributed to some of the wealth increase. New York state has a legal case in which the Trump Organization has been fined almost half a billion dollars for illegal tax evasions.

- Compared to other investments, the numbers could be more convincing. The S&P index was 2,406 in January 2000 and rose to 4,794 at the end of 2023, a 100% increase.[45] If the $1.7 billion estimated worth of assets in the Trump organization had been invested in the S&P 500 index in 2000, it would have grown to $3.4 billion by the end of 2023. This is a neat $700 million more than Forbes estimated the value of the Trump organization's assets in 2023. And if you compare with the *"big guys,"* a share in Warren Buffett's Berkshire Hathaway was $71,000 on December 29, 2000. By 2023, it had increased to $615,000, more than 700%.

This shows that Donald Trump's endless bragging about how *"I built this empire by myself"* and *"a company worth more than $10 billion"* is put to shame.

On the flip side, many heirs have wasted their inherited fortunes. Credit is due to Donald Trump for increasing the value of the Trump company. However, It is a shame that the alleged wealth is corroded by shady and sometimes illegal methods.[46]

The Apprentice. (2004-2017)

Despite many business failures in the 1980s and 1990s, Trump managed, particularly with the help of his father and through clever branding, to extend the family business. In 2004, when Donald Trump had cultivated the image of a billionaire tycoon, he joined the reality TV show *"The Apprentice."* It is estimated that this netted Trump around $200 million—a convenient sum, even for a presumable billionaire. Little did he know that this would also be

National fame from Apprentice—a political advantage:

Years of continuous nationwide exposure of Trump and the Trump brand made him a national celebrity, an image of the American dream, a self-made billionaire, and a great *"trump card"* for his presidential candidacy.

Gwenda Blair (author of "Donald Trump; Master Apprentice") notes: *"It gave him ten years of being in front of the American public as the boss, being CEO, hiring people, famously firing people, being the guy who can fix it, the one who knows everything, being the big authoritarian patriarchal guy. I think that has imprinted on a lot of people that they 'trust' him, that makes him 'trustworthy.' That, combined with the reality TV phenomenon, made it acceptable to have something that wasn't really true. It legitimized a kind of not-quite-true thing and shifted our idea of what's an acceptable version of reality."*

By coincidence, his TV reality career ended abruptly on June 16, 2015, the same day he announced his candidacy for the presidency of the U.S. How come? NBC fired him for his remarks on Mexican immigrants during his announcement. This was a somewhat controversial and unorthodox head start to a presidential campaign, to say the least! Time has shown that this was the beginning of the many controversies surrounding Trump.

Trump unexpectedly won the 2016 presidential election—but how did it happen?

Interestingly, Donald Trump shared an advantage/ disadvantage symbiosis with Ronald Reagan: both were famous nationwide on the one hand, but non-politicians, on the other hand, both were ready to *"shape up"* selfish politicians. It was the right combination at the right time for both. However, at the outset of his 2016 campaign, Trump was not given much chance.

He entered his campaign with a *"bombshell,"* calling Mexican immigrants rapists (for which NBC promptly fired him from *"The Apprentice"*) and saying he would build a wall along the Mexican border to be paid by Mexican taxpayers. These were just two of many controversial statements. Over the following years, these blunt, often rude and demeaning statements became trademarks for Trump. How could such a person become the president of the United States?

He was, perhaps unsurprisingly, met with skepticism—even mockery. The Daily News called him a clown, and hosts on CNN openly laughed at him. MSNBC and other news channels likewise gave him *"the cold shoulder."* This was probably the main reason why Trump later staged a war on the news media, repeatedly calling them *"fake news."* He was even distrusted by members of the Republican Party, who created a *"Stop Trump Movement,"* fearing that his candidacy could damage the Party's image. (How right they were.)

Throughout the campaign, he continued making polarizing statements. He received much criticism from immigrants, feminist groups, and the media, and poll numbers didn't give him much chance, showing a solid lead for the Democratic candidate, Hillary Clinton. Neither did the three presidential debates with Clinton give him an edge. Clinton also *"won"* all three by a large margin when looking at the opinion polls.[47]

Trump—a TV personality without any political background? But he won—a big surprise for most. He was simply the underdog who overcame adversity, mirroring the image created about Trump in *"The Apprentice."*

One person, though, predicted that Trump would win: Scott Adams, perhaps best known for his *"Dilbert"* books. In his book *"Win Bigly: Persuasion in a World Where Facts Don't Matter,"* he said persuasion and understanding the human mind were winning recipes. And, at least in this case, he was perfectly correct!

The 2016 presidential election numbers:

The overall votes were not in his favor. Hillary Clinton received 61 million votes against Trump's 58 million; Trump was beaten by 3 million votes. He garnered slightly fewer votes than Mitt Romney in the preceding 2012 election—and Romney lost!

So why did Trump win while Romney lost when they received a similar number of votes?

One reason was that independents and third-party voters (Libertarians and Green Party voters) *"stole"* almost 5 million more votes from the Democratic Party in 2016 than in 2012. (RFK Junior, if choosing to run, with absolutely no chance to be president, but driven by an ego, being able to say "I was a presidential candidate" could play the same damaging role for the Democrats in the 2024 election.) Another factor in 2016 was the significant shift of white voters, particularly young whites without a college education, with lower-than-average salaries, and without any strong party affiliation. This group fled from the Democratic to the Republican Party, particularly and dramatically in six swing states: Minnesota, Wisconsin, Iowa, Pennsylvania, Ohio, and Michigan. For this group, the government's perceived ability to improve their economy was decisive in 2016—and will likely be in 2024. Their personal economic situation tends to weigh more than political matters such as abortion and voting rights. The final and decisive *"punch"* in 2016 was the votes from the Electoral College. They are the ones who pick the winner.

Trump got 304 votes from 30 states, and Clinton 224 votes from 21 states.[48]

Did Donald Trump become president by sheer luck?

Or did he conquer the masses thanks to an elaborate communication style? The answer is probably both. It started with Trump's not carefully planned, unconventional, direct, and rough style. It quickly became evident that this approach could be the basis for a successful campaign—many people liked his style: fighting the elite, *"getting rid of the swamp,"* and *"I alone can fix it."* With the help of Steve Bannon and Stephen Miller, Donald Trump soon became the driver of a well-oiled campaign machine—a driver who did not seem to have much regard for speed limits.

His 2016 presidential campaign.

The reasons for Trump's surprising 2016 win can be explained by five factors: Rhetoric, Populism, Charisma, Lying, and Social Media.

The combination of these five factors played (and still plays) a big part in Trump's popularity and success.[49]

- **Rhetoric—the art of persuading an audience.** [50]

Trump has managed to persuade millions of Americans with his rhetoric. The philosopher Aristotle defined rhetoric as combining three elements: logos—facts, ethos—credibility, and pathos—emotion. However, according to Scott Adams, the businessman's success mainly rested on his power of persuasion and understanding of the human mind, not so much on facts.[51] *"Win Bigly, Persuasion in a World Where Facts Don't Matter,"*

This approach worked well for Trump, as facts are not his *"cup of tea."* He managed to circumvent the facts element by combining lies, twisted facts, and *"real"* facts into a big, confusing soup. This soup became the truth and nothing but the truth for his fans—a well-known strategy for dictators and authoritarians.

Regarding his political credibility, Trump had little to boast about at the outset of his campaign. However, he turned this to his advantage by bragging about and boosting his authority, convincing people that he, as a billionaire, was the man to run the country. *"I have the authority to run this country, just like I have run my businesses,"* he claimed. He further enhanced his credibility by diminishing that of his rivals. It was a nasty trick, but it seemed to serve him well.

As for the emotional part, it has become evident that Trump is a master at rallies. Like Hitler, he seems to rise to the occasion—Hitler with his voice and gestures, Trump with his charisma and gestures—both able to persuade their audiences to believe everything they say.

- **Populism—*"the people against the elite"* and *"permanent crisis."***

Populism also has played—and plays, a vital part in Trump's success, even though he probably has never been—nor is a populist in the proper sense. He is more focused on *"I"* than *"the people."* However, Stephen Miller and Steve Bannon addressed this early on by adjusting his speeches to focus less on himself and more on Trump's sympathy with the working class. From that point onward, Trump usually included *"the people"* in his populist rhetoric. An analysis of Trump's 73 campaign speeches underscores how cleverly Bannon, Miller, and Trump managed to work the crowd to convince them that Donald Trump was *"their man."*

"...*during the 2016 electoral campaign, we argue that his political rhetoric, which led to his presidential victory, addressed the white working class's concern with their declining position in the national pecking order. He addressed their concern by raising the moral status of this group*:

1. *Emphatically describing them as hardworking Americans who are victims of globalization;*
2. *Voicing their concerns about 'people above' (professionals, the rich, and politicians);*
3. *Drawing firm moral boundaries toward undocumented immigrants, refugees, and Muslims;*
4. *Presenting African American and (legal) Hispanic Americans as workers who also deserve jobs;*
5. *stressing the role of working-class men as protectors of women and LGBTQ people.*" [52]

• **Charisma:**

Charisma has many shades, but in a business and political sense, *"the ability to attract the attention and admiration of others and to be seen as a leader"* is a definition that fits Trump well. Trump shares this charisma not only with Hitler and other despots but also with all cult leaders, for whom charisma is an indispensable factor.

• **Lying:**

In hindsight, we learn that, according to fact-checking organizations, Trump made a record number of false statements during the campaign compared to other candidates, a pattern that continued after he became president.[53]

- **Social Media:**

From the outset of his political career, Trump has used social media to engage directly with his followers and to get media attention. By shocking social media behavior, using rough language, and making provocative statements, Trump, deliberately or not, got massive media attention to the degree that it helped him to set the media agenda.

Trump's communication strategy:

From the outset of his 2016 campaign, Trump cleverly used outrageous and controversial comments to generate news coverage. As the old saying goes: *"All publicity is good publicity."*

- He indirectly blamed George Bush for the 9/11 attack on the World Trade Center in 2001: *"He was president, okay?"*
- He demeaned John McCain: *"He's not a war hero. Is he a war hero because he was captured? I like people who weren't captured."* This must have felt disgusting for the families and friends of Vietnam veterans who knew the pain not only McCain but thousands of POWs (most of them shot down from their airplanes) had endured during the years they were imprisoned.

- In July 2015, he claimed to be a multi-billionaire: *"As of this date, my net worth is more than TEN BILLION DOLLARS."*[54]

It later became clear that Trump's claim about his net worth was largely false, as revealed by a two-year investigation by the New York Times. In March 2024, he could not come up with $460 million, either in cash or as a bond guarantee, an amount required in a New York lawsuit to have the right to appeal the verdict for financial fraud.

These *"sensational"* outbursts made headlines and, surprisingly for most at that time, did not seem to hurt his image. Almost to the contrary: here was a man unafraid to go against established norms, not afraid to talk straightforwardly—unlike the politicians. Many thought, *"He can be our man!"*

Slogans also became an essential part of Trump's election success. He started with *"Mexican immigrants are rapists,"* soon followed by *"News media are fake news,"* and cracked the code by re-inventing Reagan's slogan: *"Make America Great Again."* This was many notches better than George Bush's *"Stand by your president,"* one notch better than Obama's *"Yes, we can!"* and far better than his rival, Hillary Clinton's *"Stronger Together," "Love Trumps Hate," "I'm With Her,"* and *"I Am Ready for Hillary."*

A surprising and unexpected election win? Clearly yes! Sheer luck? Definitely no!

CHAPTER 4

HIS PRESIDENTIAL TERM 2016-2020. ACHIEVEMENTS AND FAILURES. BROKEN PROMISES

Trump brought a reality TV style into the White House, underlining his brand as an unorthodox leader capable of making quick decisions. Political enemies attacked him for his dramatic *"struggle"* narrative, but that only seemed to strengthen the ties with his base—they could identify with him: an underdog, an *"outsider"* to the political establishment but with the energy and will of a *"strongman."*

He also brought the vast promises he made before entering the White House. Did he live up to these promises? That depends, of course, on which political lens you use to view his term.

To the 74.2 million Americans who voted for Trump in 2020: It is time to check facts credibility—after claiming he could run this country. But be aware: It might lead you to change your mind about Mr. Trump.[55]

Let's start with a quick look at his policies:

Consistent with conservative Republican Party policies, Trump supported income tax cuts, deregulation, increased military spending, the appointment of conservative judges wherever possible, and efforts to limit federal healthcare protections. He introduced a harsher policy of trade protectionism, which cut across party lines, even though many of the deals could be seen as clearly nationalistic, including the stricter immigration policy where the Trump administration introduced periodic severe immigration restraints.[56]

However, Trump was far from consistent. Politico described his positions as *"eclectic, improvisational,* and often contradictory."* An NBC News count noted he made *"141 distinct shifts on 23 major issues."* Was he a man for all seasons?

Let's take a closer look at his policies and their impacts.

Achievements.

Persuading NATO partners to increase their defense spending.

On behalf of the U.S., the most powerful member and most significant economic contributor to the NATO alliance, President Trump demanded increased defense spending from European NATO partners, even before Putin attacked Ukraine. He insisted they meet the minimum of 2% of their national budgets, an agreement made by NATO partners in 2014.

European NATO countries had long been lenient, given the extended peace period since 1945, leading to stagnation in their defense budgets, most of which were well below the agreed 2%. This lack of prioritization persisted until Putin attacked Ukraine. Naïve? Yes. (Putin annexed Crimea in 2014 and had expansion plans that were ignored by Obama and the European allies.)

Thus, Trump had valid reasons for demanding higher contributions from European NATO partners. Their defense spending below 2% was not comparable to the USA's 3.5% and Russia's 4.1%. However, 2023 and 2024 have brought significant changes, with defense expenditures rapidly rising to the sound of rockets from Russia.

Warning of European energy dependence on Russia.

Trump recognized the danger of European reliance on Russian energy, explicitly pointing to the vast gas pipeline project between Russia and Germany. He advised that the funds would be better spent on defense and developing alternative energy sources. This contributed to Germany's decision to cancel the almost completed second gas pipeline from Russia to Europe and to seek alternative suppliers.

The Abraham Accords.

This agreement between Israel and three Arab countries—the United Arab Emirates, Morocco, and Sudan—represents a treaty based on mutual respect and understanding. The Trump administration played a significant role in facilitating this agreement. While these three countries were not in active conflict with Israel, the accords marked a step in the right direction. Hopefully, they will serve as a foundation for peace if and when the Israel-Hamas conflict is resolved. Until then, the accords remain a hopeful but largely symbolic gesture.

Efforts to solve the Palestinian-Israel conflict.

Trump's plan to address the Palestinian-Israeli conflict was announced on January 28, 2020, with President Trump and Israeli Prime Minister Netanyahu standing side by side, but notably without any Palestinian representatives. The plan failed to gain traction as it demanded too few concessions from the Israelis and imposed excessively harsh requirements on the Palestinians. While the plan was ultimately unsuccessful, the Trump administration should be credited for attempting to address this long-standing issue, even if the effort was politically motivated.

Reaching out to North Korea.

Trump's attempts to engage with North Korean dictator Kim Jong-un were initially seen as naive and poorly prepared by many international analysts. However, he managed to achieve some breakthroughs. Trump and Kim Jong-un met in Hanoi, Vietnam, and later in Singapore. Trump even became the first sitting U.S. president to visit North Korea. During these meetings, Kim Jong-un signed a joint statement agreeing to accelerate the denuclearization process on the Korean peninsula. However, this agreement soon proved fruitless as Kim Jong-un quickly disregarded the deal and has since signed a law stating that North Korea would never give up its nuclear weapons.

Signed the First Step Act into law in December 2018 to reform the criminal justice system.

The bill passed with overwhelming bipartisan support in Congress.

Supported the U.S. efforts in the defeat of ISIS's caliphate in 2019.

America did not engage in any new wars during the Trump administration—quite a surprising feat considering Trump's nature.

Negatives:

The Election Lie.

Not accepting a legal presidential election and inspiring an attempted coup d'état undermined one of the fundamental pillars of a functioning democracy: A peaceful transfer of power.

Poor handling of the Covid-19 pandemic.

Another disastrous one: During his final year as president, hundreds of thousands of Americans died from a pandemic that Trump deliberately downplayed to the public. Public health experts have cited Trump's light-hearted approach to the virus and his tendency not to accept science as one of the primary reasons why the US emerged as the epicenter.[57]

No replacement for the discarded Affordable Care Act.

Trump did not offer a replacement for the Affordable Care Act., In his 2016 campaign, he promised *"insurance for everybody"* and a more immediate replacement for the nearly decade-old ACA, but he never delivered.[58]

America's declining global image.

To a large part, Trump personally must be held responsible for America's declining global image, encouraging China and Russia to fill the void in global leadership.[59]

First president to be impeached twice.

Trump is the only president to be impeached twice: once for abuse of power over his dealings with Ukraine and once for obstructing the impeachment inquiry. In both cases, he was saved by the Republican Party's senators and house representatives.

Pulling US troops out of Syria.

His decision to pull US troops out of northern Syria in October 2019 is considered one of his most disastrous foreign policy moves. By doing that, Trump abandoned US-allied Kurdish forces who had been crucial to the US-led campaign against ISIS. The withdrawal created a humanitarian crisis and a security vacuum from which Russia, Iran, and Syrian President Bashar al-Assad, an accused war criminal, benefitted.

Withdrawing the U.S. from the 2015 nuclear deal.

His decision to withdraw the U.S. from the 2015 nuclear deal in 2018 remains one of Trump's most unpopular decisions. U.S. allies who also signed this deal condemned it.

Believing Putin over U.S. Intelligence.

He did not confront Putin with facts from U.S. intelligence that Russia paid bounties to Taliban-linked Afghan militants to kill U.S. troops.

Choosing Cabinet members whose aim seemed to be to undermine their departments' policy goals.

-The Secretary of Education advocated against the public school system.

-The Environmental Protection Agency (EPA) director had repeatedly sued the same EPA.

-The Attorney General helped Trump personally, undermining trust in the DOJ.

-Other departments reportedly withered from neglect, with key positions filled by unqualified people or left vacant.

Supporting conspiracy theories.

He both allowed and created conspiracy theories. Numerous examples exist; one study of his tweets found: *"136 of Trump's tweets engage the Birther and Stop the Steal conspiracy theories. I find that Trump amplifies conspiracy theories through social media and entertainment features. His emphasis on entertainment increases the embodiment of conspiracies in his followers."* [60]

Reversing important climate rules and agreements.

During his presidency, 100 environmental rules were reversed.[61]

(Disclaimer: His followers will likely put the first as well as the last three *"negatives"* on a *"positives"* list.)

Debatable:

Installed three conservative Supreme Court Justices for a lifetime appointment.

In Trump's term, Republicans also managed to appoint more than 200 judges throughout the lower courts. Most were conservative. This is a *"debatable"* achievement because of its long-term impact on judicial and political matters. Conservatives are delighted with these moves, while Democrats and liberals are not. This situation reveals a weakness in the judiciary system, where judges are often appointed based on political leanings rather than judicial competence.

The *"Tax Cuts and Jobs Act."*

A tax reform, bringing sweeping changes to the tax code, including reducing corporate taxes.[62]

-The most significant overhaul of the tax code in 30 years.

-A significant reduction of corporate tax from 35% to 21%.

-Many tax benefits to help individuals and families are temporary and will expire in 2025 and 2027.

This tax reform package was considered a victory for the wealthy, the banks, and large corporations. They were given significant and permanent tax cuts to corporate profits, investment income, and estate tax. Also, it allows a preferable tax treatment for pass-through companies.[63]

However, for the not-so-wealthy, this tax act was not a victory. The Joint Committee on Taxation estimated that the 22,000 households making $20,000 to $30,000 will collectively pay 26.6% more in 2027 than they would under the previous statute in that year. The 629 households making over $1,000,000 will pay 1% less.[64]

The tax cut bill passed in December 2017 is estimated to add about a trillion dollars to the federal deficit, forcing further restraint on future governments.

The US economy during four years with Trump:

In his re-election campaign in November 2020, Trump claimed, *"We built the greatest economy in the history of the world."* Reality paints a different picture. Trump liked to use the Dow Jones Industrial Average (the performance of 30 large companies listed on the US stock exchanges), which was unsurprising: This index grew considerably during his term as big corporations were given significant tax benefits and did quite well—until the pandemic. The most commonly used measure is overall economic growth (GDP), but numbers about job creation, inflation, and interest rates are also often used as financial indicators.

Let's have a look at those factors.

• Overall economic growth:

During Trump's first three years—before the COVID pandemic hit—the annual growth was 2.5%. According to research done by the BBC, *"…the economy was doing well prior to the pandemic … but it's clear there have been frequent periods when the growth of GDP—the value of goods and services in the economy—has been significantly higher than under President Trump. In the early 1950s, for example, the annualized GDP growth rate periodically exceeded 10%."* [65]

Overall, compared with all presidential periods after WWII, the annual GDP growth in the Trump period is below average. (The economic growth rate was pessimistic in his last year due to the pandemic, so evaluating it is unfair.)

- ## Dow Jones Stock Index:

The Dow rose at an average of almost 12% annually in Trump's first three years, better than any of his predecessors. Although it is one of many frequently used indicators, it is far from the best. "Stock prices reflect investors' best predictions about what various companies will be worth and how much those companies will produce in dividends in the future. [66]

"There is little correlation between the value of the Dow Jones index and the rate of US gross domestic product (GDP) growth. The stock market growth that defined the first three years of Trump's presidency was not felt by the average American. The investor class briefly got richer, as did those with enough money to afford significant retirement savings, while the rest of the country lived in an economy much like the one Obama left behind."[67]

The Dow fell *"back to start"* during the pandemic.

- ## Inflation:

Inflation is calculated using the U.S. Bureau of Labor Statistics consumer price index data, which measures price changes in consumer goods and services over time. The average yearly inflation rate under Trump was 2.1% in the first three years. Specifically, the consumer price index in December 2017 from 12 months earlier was 2.1%, 1.9% for the same period in 2018, 2.3% in 2019, and 1.3% in 2020. This was better than most presidents before him. The inflation rate was kept low during the pandemic due to reduced spending pressure. (There have been false statistics circulating on Facebook and Telegram, understating rates for the Trump years and significantly overstating them for Biden's administration.)[68]

- **Job Creation:**

Job creation under Trump's term was low, even before the pandemic—the lowest annual growth since 2010 and lower than the average under presidents before him since WWII. This starkly contrasts his campaign claim: *"I'll be the most significant job president God ever created. He became the first president since the Great Depression to depart office with fewer jobs in the country than when he entered. For comparison:* "Biden's four years, on the other hand, show a substantial increase in jobs created, even when excluding the unnatural boost after the pandemic. [69] [70]

- **Interest rates:**

For decades, average annual interest rates have fallen from 13.9% in 1981 to 0.9% in the pandemic year. Under Trump's administration, the average percentages for the first three years were 2.3%, 2.9%, and 2.3%. And down to 0.9% in 2020, the first pandemic year. It is not the most critical indicator for the economy, but it is pretty significant for consumers as it has a powerful impact on house loans, car loans, etc. During the three years following the pandemic, interest rates rose to 1.5%, 3%, and 3.6% because of the increased buying (and loan) pressure when the pandemic ceased.[71]

Broken promises:

Did not build a Mexican border wall with Mexican taxpayers' money.

Part of the wall was made with American taxpayers' money. (And less than 1/4 of the wall was built.)

Did not reduce the national debt.

The opposite happened. Tax cuts (corporate tax reduced from 35% to 21%), lack of spending restraint, and COVID-19 made it surge from $19 trillion when Trump took office to $28 trillion at the end of his term. The national debt increased from about $19 trillion to $23 trillion by the end of 2019—before the pandemic hit. A year of COVID-19 sent the national debt up an additional $5 trillion, now amounting to nearly $28 trillion. The total debt was now higher (30%) than GDP. *"Not since World War II has the country seen deficits during times of low unemployment that are as large as those that we project—nor, in the past century, has it experienced large deficits for as long as we project,"* Phillip Swagel, director of the CBO, said in January 2020. [72]

Did not condemn white supremacist violence.

Trump never made a swift and forceful condemnation of white supremacist violence. On the contrary, he subtly supported white supremacy.

Two of his closest advisors, Steve Bannon and Stephen Miller support the *"Great Replacement Theory,"* which fears that whites will become a powerless minority in the face of changing demographics. Politically, he has tried to tread carefully not to be labeled an extremist. But taking into account who he has picked as close advisors, his interaction with persons known for their support of white power of supremacy (Nick Fuentes, rapper Ye, and Kyle Rittenhouse), and from not denouncing groups like the Proud Boys, the Jan. 6 rioters, etc, I guess there is rightfully to say that he is a white supremacy enabler.[73]

Did not deliver significant infrastructure investments.

Infrastructure investments were made, but not at any significant level.

Did not improve protection and entitlements for older people.

He promised protection and entitlements for older people. That promise ended up in a department drawer.[74]

Historians rank Trump as the worst of all 45 presidents in the latest 2024 survey.

Every 4-year when a new president is elected, historians and experts give an evaluation, a *"ranking"* of all the 44 US presidents. It has Abraham Lincoln, George

Washington, Theodore, and Franklin Roosevelt as the top picks. And shocking fact (for all Trump fans):

This time, in 2024, Donald Trump was ranked at the bottom of all 45 presidents[75]—down from no—41 in the 2021 ranking.[76] The ranking is based on the evaluation by 154 presidential specialists who are current and recent members of the American Political Science Association. They were asked to give each president a score from 0 to 100. Trump received an average score of 11. Andrew Johnson (known for his drunkenness) and James Buchanan (blamed by contemporaries for the outbreak of the Civil War) came closest to Trump at the bottom with scores of 20 and 17, respectively. More than half of the 45 presidents received a score of over 50, with Lincoln topping the list with an average score of 94.

The criteria used as guidelines were:

- Public persuasion
- Crisis leadership
- Economic management
- Moral authority
- International relations
- Administrative skills
- Relations with Congress
- Vision/setting an agenda
- Pursued equal justice for all
- Performance within the context of the times.

Mr. Trump's best scores came for *"public persuasion,"* but he ranked last of all 45 presidents for (surprise, surprise) *"moral authority,"* among other categories. *"Newcomer"* Joe

Biden was ranked 14th. The Guardian dryly notes: *"… As for the Americans casting a ballot for the next president [in November 2024], they are in the historically rare position of knowing how both candidates have performed in the job."*

Conclusion about Donald Trump's policies and results 2016-2020:

The economic situation in Trump's first three years was decent, close to the average for the most critical economic parameters compared to other presidential periods since 1950. However, it fell far short of Trump's claim of having created the best economy in the world and is the most significant job president God ever created. Inflation and interest rates were low, while corporations and investors benefited from favorable tax reductions and tax-exempt possibilities. Unemployment was higher than usual, and job creation was low, even when excluding the COVID-19 pandemic year.

Regarding non-economic results, the fatal January 6 attack on Congress and the negligence of the COVID-19 pandemic, particularly in the first half year, as well as the anti-vaccination stance, will go down in history as paramount mistakes by Trump and his administration. To the delight of conservatives, he appointed three conservative judges to the Supreme Court and many conservative judges at lower levels. Stricter rules and regulations, some temporary, reduced the number of immigrants.

The Trump administration pushed hard against the Affordable Care Act, making it harder for people to get medical coverage by drastically cutting funding for

Medicare. These are probably the two main reasons why 3 million more people were without health insurance coverage than at the beginning of his term.

Overall, apart from primarily helping right-wing conservatives, Donald Trump did not stand out as a president for the people. Furthermore, his refusal to accept a lawful transfer of power to the lawfully elected president and his involvement in an attack on Congress does not bode well for his legacy. His boasting about being the best and most significant president in U.S. history is, at best, empty words and, at worst, flat-out lies.

CHAPTER 5

THE FALL. FROM PRESIDENT TO INSURRECTIONIST

The 2020 election numbers—a clear loss:

Joe Biden/Kamala Harris received 306 electoral votes, and Donald Trump/Mike Pence received 232 electoral votes, making Joe Biden the winner of the 2020 presidential election. Biden/Harris also won the majority of votes, 81.2 million (51.3%), against Trump/Pence, 74.2 million votes (46.9%).[77]

Four candidates qualified to run for the election. Besides Biden and Trump, Howie Hawkins from the Green Party and Jo Jorgensen from the Libertarian Party also participated. However, Hawkins and Jorgensen were not serious contenders: Hawkins received 0 electoral votes and 0.4 million popular votes, while Jorgensen received 0 electoral votes and 1.8 million popular votes.

Trump is refusing to accept the loss.

However, Trump contested the results from day one, claiming the election was *"stolen"* from him due to election fraud. It turns out that months before the election date when the poll numbers were not convincing for Trump, he began hinting about election fraud. And when the election numbers showed Biden as the winner, he launched a real crusade to convince people that the election had been rigged. His *"Big Election Lie"* was in motion, supported by many influential Republican leaders: Mitch McConnell, Kevin McCarthy, Josh Hawley, Ted Cruz, Joe Jordan, Andrew Clyde, Paul Gosar, and many others. Without their initial, and for most of them, continued support of Trump's election lie, Trump would likely not have been able to convince millions of Americans to believe his falsehood.

Trump tasked his legal team with challenging the election results in 61 court cases. All were lost, except one where observers had been held away from the voting stations at a distance longer than prescribed.

The Jan 6, 2021, attack on Congress.

On January 6, 2021, modern American history took a dark turn. Democracy faced a severe assault. Not since the Civil War had such audacity been witnessed in U.S. history. That day, spurred by appeals from Trump and other influential right-wing figures, the Capitol Building came under attack. Over 2,000 Trump supporters stormed the Capitol, seeking to overturn Trump's defeat in the 2020 presidential election by disrupting the certification of President-elect Joe Biden's victory by the U.S. Senate and House of Representatives.

It quickly became apparent that this was not a spontaneous effort to *"stop the steal"* but a meticulously planned attempt to seize presidential power unlawfully. This failed coup d'état served as a stark reminder to Americans of the fragility and value of their democracy, emphasizing that democracy cannot be taken for granted. On that day, the U.S. teetered on the brink of transitioning from a stable democracy to an authoritarian regime. With the aid of an incited crowd, encouraged by Trump and his allies, an attempt was made to undermine the democratic electoral process.

Thousands of Trump supporters stormed the U.S. Capitol as Congress and Vice President Mike Pence convened to count the electoral votes confirming Mr. Biden's victory. Amid the chaos, House and Senate members, along with administration officials, were compelled to evacuate as the crowd breached police barricades and infiltrated Congress. The violent clashes resulted in the deaths of five individuals and numerous injuries. Shockingly, it was revealed that members of the Proud Boys had intentions to harm Speaker of the House Nancy Pelosi, while outside, a crowd incited by Trump's speech erected a gallows, chanting *"Hang Mike Pence."*

In the aftermath, hundreds have been arrested and prosecuted for their involvement in the insurrection.

During the early stages of the attack, President Trump was implored by House Minority Leader Kevin McCarthy to intervene and call off the insurgents. Trump's response was dismissive, stating, *"They seem more interested in the election than you are."* Despite urgent pleas from numerous individuals close to him, including his children, Eric and Ivanka Trump, Fox reporters Sean Hannity and Laura Ingraham, and Capitol Hill staff, Trump remained unresponsive. All these messages were directed to Trump as the perceived instigator of the Capitol attack, yet he chose to ignore every single one of them.

Eyewitnesses recount Trump's apparent delight in watching the live coverage of the insurrection, with no intention of halting the violence. Only after repeated urging from his closest advisors did Trump reluctantly issue a tepid plea for the rioters to disperse three hours after the siege began, even adding, *"I love you."* By the time the siege ended, one person had died, and numerous others were gravely injured.

Did Trump incite the Jan 6, 2021, insurrection?

After the January 6, 2021, attack on the Capitol, more than one thousand individuals who participated have been charged with federal crimes in the riot—from misdemeanor offenses like trespassing to felonies like assaulting police officers and some for seditious conspiracy. About 500 have been sentenced to prison, ranging from a few days to 22 years.

But what about *"the boss"*—Donald Trump? The bipartisan Congressional investigation committee and several state courts found enough evidence of his active role in inciting the attack. But as of mid-2024—three and a half years after the attack—the "boss", the one who incited the whole thing—has managed to delay court trials.

Wild ego trip or carefully elaborated plan?

The media initially used terms such as *"riot," "insurrection,"* and *"attack on Congress."* However, subsequent evidence indicated that this was not a spontaneous event but a planned and failed coup d'état orchestrated by Donald Trump and executed by some of his closest allies. As this book progresses, further details are revealed, pointing to clear sedition acts. The entire scenario was a toxic mix of meticulous planning by Trump's allies, incited *"foot soldiers,"* and one man's refusal to accept the results of a legitimate election.

However, Trump and his team of lawyers claim that he is *"immune"* and have succeeded in bringing the case to the Supreme Court.

This case exemplifies how a seemingly simple, logical case can be twisted into a complicated judicial matter. The decision by the Supreme Court in this case will be crucial in determining whether Donald Trump will be allowed to continue his attempt to ride toward autocracy.

One could ask: Why this frantic opposition to a legally conducted election? Ben-Ghiat, a professor of history and Italian studies at New York University, said. *"He's an authoritarian, and they can't leave office. They don't have good endings, and they don't leave properly."* [78]

No fraud that could change the election result was found. Despite this, Trump and his allies did not give up and continued not only to spread the baseless lie about election fraud but also to take active measures:

- They actively tried to illegally change the result by using fake elector teams.
- They demanded and were granted recounts in multiple states, all showing that the election results were valid.
- Donald Trump personally requested that Georgia State Secretary Brad Raffensperger find 11,000 votes to win the Georgia election. Raffensperger recounts the episode in his book *"Integrity Counts,"* stating that Trump's order seemed like a demand to do as he said—or else. *"I felt then—and still believe today—that this was a threat."*

All these illegal attempts culminated in the January 6, 2021, attack on Congress, an effort to stop the counting of the electoral votes, which is the formal procedure to confirm Biden's win.

Who were the people supporting Trump strongly enough to engage in violent actions like this?

About 800 rioters broke into the Capitol. A survey of 420 people arrested or charged shows that 96% were white and 83% were male.[79]

Two-thirds were over 34 years old, predominantly in their early 40s, most having families and stable jobs. Notably, 45% held significant roles, such as CEOs, business owners, doctors, lawyers, accountants, or mid-level managers. Only 7% were unemployed, and fewer than 10% had affiliations with militant groups.

Ten million Americans willing to participate in a violent protest?

Soon after the attack on Congress, 1,000 representative Americans were surveyed with the following questions:

"Do you think the election was stolen?"
"Would you willingly participate in a violent protest?"

Remarkably, 4%—about 10 million people—responded that they would participate in a violent protest. These individuals are supporters of Trump's increasingly threatening rhetoric.

The white replacement theory.

The notion that the rights of Hispanics and Blacks surpass those of Whites played a significant role.

Three studies employing varied methodologies revealed that counties experiencing a notable percentage decline in their non-Hispanic white populations were more likely to produce insurrectionists than others. The more significant the proportion of the non-Hispanic white population in a county, the higher the number of insurrectionists it produced.

First reactions among Republican and Democrat Congress representatives.

In the weeks and months following the insurrection, investigations revealed that Trump and his allies for months leading up to the event, had been meticulously planning ways to keep him in power—with stopping the electoral vote counting as just one strategy. It is perhaps unsurprising that he watched the riot unfold in real-time without intervening, only reluctantly issuing an appeal for the rioters to withdraw as the situation escalated out of control.

However, Congress resumed the interrupted formal presidential confirmation in the early hours of January 7. Vice President Pence declared Joe Biden the president with an electoral vote of 306 to Trump's 232 votes. (Total popular vote: Biden/Harris 81,283,485; Trump/Pence 74,223,774 votes.) The attack was universally condemned by leaders from both sides of the legislative aisle—Democratic and Republican—and the press, which had ample video footage of the event, having "filmed in action" by various media outlets.

Just after the attack and in the weeks that followed, both Republicans and Democrats—and the press—expressed anger and frustration. In a speech on the Senate floor, Republican Senator Graham stated emphatically, "Count me out. I have had enough," adding, *"I am sad to see this journey with Trump end this way."* Two days later, Graham expressed his dismay further, saying, *"I've never been so humiliated and embarrassed for the country."* Republican Minority Leader of the House, Kevin McCarthy, also spoke out strongly on the House floor: *"The president bears responsibility for Wednesday's attack on Congress by mob rioters. He should have immediately denounced the mob when he saw what was unfolding."* Meanwhile, the Republican Minority Leader of the Senate, Mitch McConnell, reportedly told staffers in his Capitol office that Trump was a *"despicable human being"* whom he would oppose politically.

The Republicans' "rescue plan."

Denouncing Trump's role in the Jan 6 insurrection, saving him from impeachment, and affirming they wanted to keep him as the leader of the Republican Party.

After initially distancing themselves from Trump's attempts to overturn the peaceful transition of power, Republican leadership shifted their focus toward party tactics rather than moral principles, eventually downplaying the event's significance. There were two crucial turning points: McCarthy's infamous visit to Mar-al-Lago on January 28 and McConnell's successful efforts to acquit Trump in the impeachment trial. A 180-degree turnaround operation had begun: McCarthy now started blaming Democratic House Leader Nancy Pelosi for the Capitol attack, shifting his focus entirely away from Trump. (FactCheck.org stated later, on July 29, 2021, "Attempt to Cast Blame on Pelosi for January 6. No evidence.") [80]

Days after voting to acquit Trump, McConnell stated that he would support Trump as president if he were the Republican nominee again: *"The nominee of the party? Absolutely."*

These actions and statements from McConnell and McCarthy, the two most powerful Republican leaders in Congress, effectively kick-started the party leadership's efforts to downplay the event.

They fiercely refused to form a Congressional investigation committee. The resistance was, again, led by the two Mc's in the Senate: McConnell and McCarthy. Despite the resistance, a bipartisan committee was appointed, with two members from the Republican Party and six from the Democratic Party. (After the Democrats offered a 50/50 representation but refused to accept two insurrection deniers into the committee initially proposed by the Republicans.)

And from there, Republican downplaying and direct denial of the January 6 event rolled on:

- The influential RNC (The Republican National Committee), on February 5, called the insurrection a *"legitimate political discourse."* [81]
- The No. 3 House Republican, Elise Stefanik, copied McCarthy and falsely blamed Pelosi for the violence on January 6. *"The American people deserve to know the truth: that Nancy Pelosi bears responsibility, as speaker of the House, for the tragedy that occurred on January 6."*
- Andrew Clyde, a Republican congressman representing Georgia, infamously said that the rioters looked like *"a normal tourist visit."* A statement that has since been much deservedly ridiculed. The same bizarre sentiment was echoed by

- Tucker Carlson of Fox News who argued *that "the vast majority of people inside the Capitol on January 6 were peaceful*

  … You see people walking around and taking pictures. They don't look like terrorists, but tourists, and all of them, by the way, are Americans… They weren't trying to overthrow the government."

  Michael Fanone, the Police Officer who almost lost his life defending the Capitol on Jan. 6. said later in an interview with the magazine Rolling Stones: *"There was the moment when it became clear that reality didn't actually fucking matter to Trump's apologists and acolytes."*

  "You call [Jan. 6] a 'tourist day. You say it was 'hugs and kisses.' I'm going to be that fucking inconvenient motherfucker that pops his head up every time you say some stupid shit like that."

- Arizona representative Paul Gosar did his part in the downplay scheme: *"The Justice Department,"* he said, *"is harassing peaceful patriots across the country,"* showing his indignation that federal prosecutors filed charges against hundreds of people who stormed the Capitol and participated in the riot.

The inspirator of the march to the Capitol, Donald Trump, said in a July 2021 Fox News interview, *"The crowd was unbelievable, and I mentioned the word 'love.' The love in the air—I've never seen anything like it,",* calling the rioters *"patriots"* and *"peaceful."* And has later (in 2023) stated that Jan 6, 2021, *"was a beautiful day."*

It could be tempting to call them delusionists,[82] but I am afraid it is worse than that: They probably knew better (my guess, not verifiable!) [83]

They obviously *"forgot"* that these rioters, by their own choice, participated in an attempted coup to overturn the result of the 2020 presidential election, which is a severe crime. To make matters worse, many of the rioters were armed. The most extreme was a group called *"The Oath Keepers,"* who were dressed for combat, armed with pistols and rifles, and had a clear plan of how to take control of the situation once inside the Capitol. (At the time of writing, Stewart Rhodes, leader of the far-right militia *"The Oath Keepers,"* has been arrested and charged along with ten others with seditious conspiracy over what prosecutors said was their wide-ranging plot to storm the Capitol on January 6 last year and disrupt the certification of Biden's electoral victory.)

Intelligent individuals like Tucker Carlson set dangerous precedents by downplaying this event using misleading examples. As seen in numerous videos and told by numerous witnesses, the facts reveal gravity. Such hazardous and appalling attempts to distort and twist recent history, using the reach and power of social media, are one of the most significant challenges the U.S. faces today in the fight for democracy and truth.

The Jan 6 aftermath.

The bipartisan investigation uncovered alarming insights from numerous witnesses, revealing that this was not an impromptu attack but a well-planned coup attempt.

The inauguration week could have proceeded as usual but was marked by heavy security, including the deployment of 25,000 National Guard members. This led to the House passing a $1.9 billion *"Capitol Security Bill."*

More than three years later, destructive political fires still torment the country, causing despair and unhappiness for millions of Americans. It's important to note that the January 6 Insurrection didn't happen on a whim but was the natural result of decades of increasing political division in the U.S. However, it was inflamed by Trump and his cult of followers, fueled by social media and broadcast outlets like Fox News.

Trump received a subpoena to testify before Congress, but he and his accomplices refused to comply. Two of them (Eastman and Bannon) were charged with contempt of Congress and had to serve jail time. And Trump? He still hasn't been held accountable for any of his actions, while his accomplices and supporters have been indicted en masse and are either serving jail time or facing court trials. But Trump continues to evade court trials as he and his legal team have managed to obtain delays. However, mounting evidence of his active role in the coup attempt has been presented, and he is set to be tried in three different court cases. And this is a man who, still endorsed by the Republican Party and believed by 40% of Americans, might be President of the U.S. in 2024. Scary!

Donald Trump's visible changes in behavior after the election loss:

Donald Trump's behavior started changing following his 2020 election loss. He went from bragging and being rude, which some called *"refreshing,"* to growing increasingly sinister and mean.

Frequent use of derogatory, even hateful language.

According to Oscar Winberg, Trump's mocking and insulting rhetoric in his 2016 campaign fit into a long tradition of insult-laden political discourse. However, he said that Trump probably won the White House despite his mock rhetoric, not because of it. But he could escape it because of his political position and media image.[84]

His consistent use of hate and fear-inducing rhetoric, dismissing experts, demeaning and eliminating opponents, is precisely the strongman tactics used by Hitler, Mussolini, Lenin, Stalin, Putin, Pinochet, Orban—and Trump.[85]

Pejorative nicknames and constant use of contemptuous, demeaning behavior towards opponents or laws that were against him.

Trump consistently uses a slur of pejorative nicknames when describing others.

Wikipedia cites a list of such nicknames.[86]The list is extensive, with nearly 200 nicknames for U.S. and foreign citizens, organizations, and TV programs! This includes his famous *"China Virus"* about the virus that caused COVID-19 and *"Sleepy Joe"* about President Joe Biden.

Among these 200 nicknames, only a few are positive, such as:

Mr. Tough Guy (John Bolton)
Beautiful Ted (Ted Cruz)
Tropical Trump (Jair Bolsonaro, right-wing
    former President of Brazil)
Alexander the Great (Alexander Ovechkin,
    Russian ice hockey player and Washington
    Capitals team captain)
Sir Charles (Charles Goldstein, real estate lawyer)

However, the negative characteristics vastly outnumber the few positive ones. The most common terms include *"Crazy"* (8 times), *"Little"* (7 times), and *"Wacky"* (5 times). He frequently uses other primarily insulting terms like *"Psycho," "Stupidest," "Lyin'," "Slimeball," "Weirdo," "Low-IQ,"* and *"Crooked."*

Is this language worthy of a former president for all Americans? I don't think so. It bears the mark of a divisive language—designed not to unite a nation but to fracture it further.

Some examples of how Trump describes others:

- **Americans Who Died in War**: *"Losers"* and *"Suckers."* In a conversation with senior staff members on the morning of a scheduled visit to the Aisne-Marne American Cemetery near Paris,

Trump said, *"Why should I go to that cemetery? It's filled with losers."* The visit was canceled. In another conversation on the same trip, Trump mocked the more than 1,800 marines who lost their lives at Belleau Wood, calling them "suckers" for getting killed (The Atlantic, September 4, 2020).

- **Joe Biden**: *"Corrupt,"* *"Crooked."* Said on several occasions.
- **Senator Ted Cruz**: *"Lyin' Ted."*
- **Senator Marco Rubio:** *"Little Marco."*
- **Retired General Milley**: *"Milley is lazy; he's a lazy guy and not very smart."*
- **Former President Barack Obama:** Trump falsely claimed that Obama was not born in the U.S., expressing "doubts" in a series of interviews about Obama's birthplace and suggesting that his birth certificate might list his religion as Muslim. (Obama is Christian).

Trump's opinions and statements: (Some weird, some scary.) Some might be meant as jokes—but are they?

- In a phone call with Health and Human Services Secretary Alex Azar, Trump reportedly declared: *"Testing is killing me! I am going to lose the election because of Testing! What idiot had the federal government do Testing?"* Azar responded, *"Uh, do you mean Jared?"*
- He allegedly joked that Covid would hopefully *"take out"* Bolton.

- Another is about handling Americans who had been infected with Covid-19 abroad. *"Don't we have an island we own? What about Guantánamo?"* The idea was quickly forgotten—and scuttled when Trump brought it up again.[87]

- At an early stage of the Covid pandemic, he suggested, *"Has anyone tried injecting bleach?"*

- Bob Woodward, journalist and author, asked Trump if he had sympathy for the grievances of underprivileged Americans. *"I'm not feeling the love,"* Trump glowered, angry that populism had not guaranteed popularity (from Woodward's book *"Rage"*).

- His response to security at the *"Stop the Steal"* rally on January 6, when people with weapons were not allowed in: *"Let them in; they are not going to hurt me."*

- He is quoted saying that he could stand on New York's Fifth Avenue *"and shoot somebody"* and still not lose voters. Maybe it is a joke, or perhaps he is dead serious. Who knows.

- During the racial justice protests in June 2020, President Trump was ushered into a bunker under the White House. Shortly after, he learned that the episode had been leaked to the press. *'Whoever did that, they should be charged with treason!'* Trump yelled, according to Bender. *'They should be executed!'*[88]

Knowing that leading psychiatrists describe Trump as having a narcissistic personality and paranoid personality, it is difficult to determine if Trump meant all of this.

These statements are not the exception but have become a standard part of Trump's social media posts and political rallies. And after the 2020 election loss, Donald Trump's rhetoric has grown more and more ominous. Consider below some of the other statements he has made:

Donald Trump's threats and insults are numerous and increasing in force.

Poll workers were accused of fraud by Donald Trump and Rudy Giuliani. As a result, these poll workers received a storm of threats from MAGA supporters and felt their lives were endangered after unfounded public accusations of tampering with the ballots.

Mike Pence, his former vice president, was blamed for not helping him overturn the 2020 election results. When parading toward the Capitol on January 6, Trump's tweets to his fans that Pence *"didn't dare to do what should have been done"* prompted the MAGA supporters to raise a gallows while chanting *"Hang Mike Pence."*

Colin Kaepernick, the former NFL quarterback who protested police brutality by kneeling during the national anthem, was mocked by Trump, who said anyone who did that should be *"fired"* and called him a *"son of a bitch."*

General Mark Milley. Trump, on his social-media network, Truth Social, wrote that Milley's phone call to reassure China in the aftermath of the storming of the Capitol on January 6, 2021, was "an act so egregious that, in times gone by, the punishment would have been DEATH." (The phone call had been authorized by Trump administration officials.)

Judges and prosecutors, prime targets of Trump's anger. *"If you go after me, I'm coming after you." "You ought to go after this Attorney General." "He should rot in hell."*

Are these direct threats from a mafia boss? No, they are posts and statements done by the Republican Party's leading candidate for the presidency of the United States. Unbelievable? No, facts.

From the outside of the U.S., I can hardly believe what I see and hear from Trump, who now seems more and more unhinged. I have no other words to describe this bizarre reality unfolding in front of our eyes. This prominent presidential candidate flatly refuses to accept routine justice procedures, flatly threatens political opponents, and openly say he will seek revenge against those who worked with him but dared to go against his wishes. This behavior is a stark warning sign of what Donald Trump has in mind if he becomes the next president. Scary, chilling, and not the least worthy of a political leader in a democratic country. Where are you, Americans?

Violence in Trump's footsteps:

These are some examples of individuals and groups harassed by Trump (note that there are more people, many more, that Donald Trump has harassed. NB! This list is from 2015 to 2021. After that, the harassment rate likely increased. [89]

- The Republican National Committee
- Tony Schwartz, author of The Art of the Deal
- The Washington Post
- The New York Times
- America, if he loses the election
- Women who accuse him of sexual assault
- John McCain, the late senator from Arizona
- Megyn Kelly, former Fox News anchor
- Bill Maher, comedian and TV host
- Laurence Tribe, Harvard law professor
- Mac Miller, late rapper
- Univision
- NBC
- CNN
- Angela Merkel, chancellor of Germany
- Iran
- NATO
- The World Health Organization
- The United Nations
- The Electoral College
- Michael Cohen, former personal lawyer
- Mary Trump, niece
- John Bolton, former national security adviser
- Anthony Scaramucci, former White House communications director
- Omarosa Manigault Newman, former White House aide
- Michael Wolff, author of Fire and Fury

- Stormy Daniels, adult film star
- Jeff Bezos, founder of Amazon
- Rosie O'Donnell, actress and comedian
- Alec Baldwin, actor and SNL impersonator
- Snoop Dogg, rapper and actor
- Meryl Streep, actress
- LeBron James, NBA player
- Stephen Curry, NBA player
- The NFL
- The NBA
- Twitter
- Facebook
- Google
- TikTok

Don't tell me this man is not inflicting an atmosphere of menace and foul language upon a nation! This is not even a complete list, as there are incidents that were not reported or documented—and new ones are emerging all the time. Trump's threats have generally been empty or baseless. Still, his devoted fans see many of these insults as an invitation to act, resulting in direct threats and intimidations to the persons mentioned by Trump.[90]

We are witnessing a former president acting like a rude, immature teenager. But he is not a rude, immature teenager; he is an influential national figure with a powerful political position and fanbase willing to go to great lengths to please their cult leader. They see it almost as their duty to act on his threats on his behalf. They take his verbal attacks literally, putting the targeted individuals in real danger for their and their families' safety because of threatening letters, emails, phone calls, and more from Trump's followers. Death threats are not uncommon. Some of these targeted individuals were forced to move from their homes to a safer place, some needed police protection and all of them felt unsafe, living in fear day and night. This is because the former President of the U.S., now Mr. Donald Trump, has indicated they deserve no better. How did Trump react when he heard all the reports of victims being threatened by his followers? Silence. Remorse? Absent.

His insults and threats have developed from childish, almost funny characteristics of political opponents to baseless, mean, and dangerous threats directed not only at individuals but also at institutions and representatives of the law.

In this way, he is undermining the trust a democratic society needs to have in its institutions. The Department of Justice, the FBI, the judiciary system with judges, courts, and district attorneys—everything and anything that stands in his way—is attacked as *"corrupted," "useless," "witch hunts,"* etc., creating an image of ineffective institutions. When even intelligent people like billionaire O'Leary are dancing to the tune of Trump's tirades, I see a real danger coming.

Is Trump acting like a Mafia boss?

Some years ago, Donald Trump stated: *"Why take the Fifth if you are innocent?"* and *"Only the mob takes the Fifth."*

What happened later, when he started facing investigations for alleged fraud and crimes? He pleaded the Fifth. Not once, not twice, but repeatedly, just like *"only the mob"* does.

This mob-like behavior, not only by pleading the Fifth but by issuing indirect threats to people he does not like, has earned him a lot of suggestive nicknames that, not surprisingly, reflect his language:

"Orange Capone," "Don," "Teflon Don," "Don the Con," "Donny boy," "Donny," "Donnie," "Tfg," "The former guy," "Frump," "Drumpf," "Commander in Grift," "Doodie," "Loser," "slippery," "Lying con," "Sore-one the Loser," "Bunker boy," "the Bully," "iQ45," "Cult leader," "A pimple in the butt," "President Golfball," "Slump," "Trump stooges," and *"Trumpanzee."*

Undoubtedly, there are many more; those are the ones I have picked up in recent years.

On a personal note, I would like to add two: *"Big Liar Trump,"* and *"Lord of the Lies."*

Name glitches.

In the presidential race in 2024, it looks like there will be two *"elderly"* men: Biden and Trump. One has passed 80 years already; the other one is coming close. For most people at that age, the memory can slip at times. Both Biden and Trump have shown signs of that, which possibly, but not necessarily mean that their cognitive function is reduced. However, very lately, there seems to be a difference: Both of them have *"slips"* that seem age-related, while more and more of Trump's slips might be due to a cognitive decline, says three mental illness experts.[91] Other experts caution about conclusions: "Cognitive assessments can only be made by doctors via special in-person examinations and tests."[92] Trump has been particularly aggressive and not missed any occasions to point to *"sleepy Joe's"* slip of the tongue when Biden miss-pronounced/forgot names.

Admittedly, it's not always straightforward; Trump often struggles with names like Netanyahu (see under.)

But these gaffes do raise questions about his competency. Consider some of the following blunders he has made—here is a short list of Trump stumbling when meeting or talking about people:

- *"Tim Apple"* (Tim Cook, CEO of Apple),
- *"Steve"* (Kevin McCarthy, House of Representatives Minority Leader),
- *"Mike Bolton"* (John Bolton, senior advisor to Trump),
- *"Mike Pounds"* (Mike Pence, Vice President of the US),
- *"Jim Perry"* (Rick Perry, who served as the 14th United States Secretary of Energy from 2017 to 2019 and as the 47th Governor of Texas from 2000 to 2015),
- *"Rick Gates"* (Matt Gaetz, Republican Congressman),
- *"Netanyoo"* (Benjamin Netanyahu, Israeli Prime Minister).

CHAPTER 6

HIS PERSONALITY AND BEHAVIOR. NARCISSIST OR NOT?

Narcissist, unfit to be president?

Experts observing Donald Trump's behavior, particularly over the past decade, have grown increasingly worried and frustrated about his mental health. His upbringing, which was far from harmonious, has undoubtedly impacted him significantly. The crucial question remains: How profound is that impact?

Allegations suggest that Trump exhibits narcissistic traits or even suffers from a mental disorder. Concerns and warnings have come from mental health professionals, people who have worked closely with him, journalists, and many others. Trump's increasingly alarming behavior is a pressing issue that could influence American and global politics. How concerned should we be? Extremely.

Being a narcissist—a mental disorder?

Let me start by offering a standard description of narcissism: *"Narcissism comprises a set of defenses that protect an individual from feeling small, insignificant, and worthless. The classic narcissist is presented as grandiose, loud, pompous, and condescending. In narcissism, there's room for only one person, one 'self.' Therefore, narcissism often resembles the classic grade school behavior of belittling others to feel more significant."*

Narcissism, selfish behavior, is not necessarily a mental disorder, although the borderline might be challenging to define.

According to The American Psychiatric Association (APA), Narcissistic Personality Disorder (NPD) can only be diagnosed if a personal examination has been conducted by a mental health professional with proper authorization. APA also told its members (in March 2017, shortly after Trump became president) that it is unethical for a psychiatrist to offer **any** professional opinion unless they have conducted such an examination. (Referring to *"The Goldwater Rule."*) [93]

This last part has been contested by many of its members, who argue it acts like a *"gag order,"* restricting those with the most professional expertise from commenting on the mental health of public figures. In the case of Trump, his behavior was so alarming that some felt it was unethical NOT to raise concerns.

That same year, in 2017, a group of mental health professionals gathered at a *"Duty to Warn"* conference. It published their opinions in the book, *"The Dangerous Case of Donald Trump. 27 Psychiatrists and Mental Health Experts Assess a President."* [94]

In the book, they analyze Donald Trump's public statements and actions to illustrate their professional concerns about his psychological state. **Dr. Bandy Lee, a forensic psychiatric specialist** and the book's editor, expressed in an interview on *"Democracy Now!"* that Trump has shown an attraction to violence as a coping strategy. *"As psychiatrists, we knew that when Trump became president, he would not have the mental capacity to handle a crisis maturely. He had no grounding, no ideology that binds normal people, and he was incapable of genuinely caring about others,"* she stated.

Considering Trump's behavior following his 2020 election loss and beyond, it is crucial and timely to reflect on Dr. Bandy Lee's observation: *"Whenever the Goldwater Rule is mentioned, we should recall the Declaration of Geneva, which mandates that physicians speak out against destructive governments,"* Lee asserts. *"This declaration was formulated in response to the atrocities of Nazism."*

This seems to be a very relevant and essential observation. To put a complete restriction on mental health professionals for publicly saying anything about the mental health and behavior of possibly dangerous leaders reminds me more of *"snillism"* [95] (Norwegian; too lenient, softhearted) than realism. The debate among mental health professionals is still ongoing. Despite this *"gag order,"* numerous allegations and concerns about Trump's behavior and mental health have surfaced since he entered the political scene in 2015.

However, due to the Goldwater Rule, mental health professionals often avoid using the term *"Narcissistic Personality Disorder"* when expressing their concerns about a man whose behavior appears reminiscent of narcissism to an extent that is considered dangerous for the U.S. as a nation. Before delving into why mental health professionals are issuing warnings about Donald Trump, let's first explore their most significant concern: Trump's increasingly evident narcissistic behavior and why such behavior is causing so much concern.

Psychologist Craig Malkin delineates narcissism as *"the drive to feel special and stand out in some way from the other 8 billion people on the planet."* He further categorizes narcissism into four categories. The third category encompasses individuals who exhibit higher levels of moderate narcissism but do not reach the threshold of a diagnosable disorder. According to Malkin, they *"might be healthy, but they still are far enough up on the trait to be called a narcissist."*

"Narcissistic Personality Disorder, he says, is the final category," When levels of narcissism become disruptive enough to meet the bar of a mental health condition. People with pathological narcissism *"are so driven to self-enhance or feel special that they set aside love, connection, [and] care."* [96]

While there may be slight variations, there is significant consensus on the core traits.

Dr. Zachary Rosenthal from Duke Health offers a succinct definition, utilizing the acronym "SPECIAL ME" to aid in recalling the traits of Narcissistic Personality Disorder (NPD):

"SPECIAL ME": [97]

- Self-importance
- Preoccupation with power, beauty, or success
- Entitlement
- Preference for associating only with individuals deemed necessary or special
- Interpersonally exploitative for personal gain
- Arrogance
- Lack of empathy
- Craving admiration
- Envy of others or belief that others are envious of them

According to Dr. Rosenthal, an individual consistently exhibiting at least five of the SPECIAL ME traits meets the diagnostic criteria for the condition.

Let me quote **Allen Frances, Professor Emeritus of Psychiatry and Behavioral Sciences**, who makes a clear distinction between narcissism and Narcissistic Personality Disorder (NPD). He concludes:

"Many have mislabeled President Trump with the diagnosis of Narcissistic Personality Disorder. I authored the criteria defining this disorder, and Mr. Trump does not meet them. He may be a world-class narcissist, but this does not make him mentally ill because he does not suffer from the distress and impairment necessary to diagnose a mental disorder.

*Mr. Trump **causes** severe distress rather than experiencing it and has been richly rewarded, rather than punished, for his grandiosity, self-absorption, and lack of empathy. ...Bad behavior* *is rarely a sign of mental illness, and the mentally ill misbehave only seldom."* [98]

Donald Trump is a prominent figure, and his behavior is constantly on display through TV appearances, interviews, political rallies, written statements, and more. However, mental health professionals are instructed to use the term NPD only after conducting a personal examination of the individual in question. For those of us observing from the outside, it is natural to speculate based on what we see, hear, and experience. Equipped with the above *"Special Me"* definition, we may be able to make more informed assessments.

Given Trump's behavior and his position as a potential leader of an entire nation, speculation about his mental health is inevitable. However, as someone outside of Trump's circle, I am less qualified to judge his mental health. Nonetheless, outsiders often offer unique perspectives on situations. From my vantage point, Trump appears to meet five of the above nine criteria, with the remaining four being highly probable.

It is essential to recognize the fine but distinct line between being on the higher end of narcissism and having a narcissistic personality disorder. As mentioned earlier, diagnosing narcissism as a mental disorder should be the exclusive purview of qualified mental health professionals conducting personal examinations. I believe such an examination has not been conducted in Donald Trump's case, so it is prudent to set that definition aside for now.

However, Trump's level of narcissism appears to have intensified following the election loss and in response to the pressures stemming from his numerous legal encounters. Recently, his speeches have seemed more disjointed, leading experts to cite this as a potential sign of cognitive decline. Consequently, concerns regarding Trump's mental health and behavior are on the rise.

There is also considerable apprehension surrounding President Joe Biden's cognitive health. Both Trump and Biden are at an age where cognitive abilities may diminish. However, unlike Trump, Biden appears to be focused on serving the American people, while Trump remains primarily self-absorbed—a crucial distinction, in my opinion. The contrast in their behavior is stark.

Nevertheless, in the early months of 2024, both candidate Trump and President Biden displayed disturbing signs of speech issues that were noticeable to all. This may become a sensitive issue as the year progresses.

Let's listen to some other mental health professionals share their worries about Trump:

As far back as 2015, when Donald Trump began his political journey as a presidential candidate, there were already warnings about his personality.

Joseph Burgo, a licensed clinical psychologist, said in August 2015: "To describe Donald Trump as a narcissist has become cliché, so widely accepted that the use of the label barely raises an eyebrow. ... Extreme narcissists like Donald Trump rely on a characteristic set of defenses to evade painful truths about themselves and to shore up that inflated sense of self: righteous anger, blame, and contempt." [99]

In November of that same year, prominent mental health professionals participated in a panel discussion, expressing their deep concern about a possible Trump presidency and warning about his personality and behavior. (Notably, none of these professionals diagnosed Trump with Narcissistic Personality Disorder, but some made comparisons.)

"Remarkably narcissistic," said **developmental psychologist Howard Gardner,** a Harvard Graduate School of Education professor.

Clinical psychologist Ben Michaelis noted Trump's bullying nature, such as taunting Senator John McCain for being captured in Vietnam, which aligns with a narcissistic profile. Michaelis added, *"He's applying for the greatest job in the land, the greatest task of which is to serve. Still, there's nothing about the man that is service-oriented. He's only serving himself."*

Clinical psychologist George Simon remarked, *"He's so classic that I'm archiving video clips of him to use in workshops because there's no better example of his characteristics."*

One of the mental health professionals in the panel, Mr. Gardner, touched on a broader, even more scary scope: *"For me, the compelling question is the psychological state of his supporters. They are unable or unwilling to make a connection between the challenges faced by any president and the knowledge and behavior of Donald Trump. In a democracy, that is disastrous."* [100]

Many colleagues share these concerns.

Bill Eddy, Co-Founder and President of the High Conflict Institute and author of the book *"Why We Elect Narcissists and Sociopaths—and How We Can Stop,"* [101] *"First, he has a highly conflicted personality and a fixation on lying to others. He has narcissistic traits like being preoccupied with himself. He has superb ideas with no basis for them. He seems to lack empathy. His goal is to be seen as the most superior person in the world, always stepping on people to get higher and higher. He has sociopathic traits, like being highly aggressive. He is willing to take risks that everyone is shocked at. And then he gets away with it, and even he is surprised. But also deceitful, lying, and cunning. Also, a lack of remorse and a drive to domi-nate other people. And this is what you see in other authoritarian leaders around the world. They divide people, put up fences, and like to have the power to make people do things they don't want. I see Hitler, Stalin, and Mao as the originals. … It's not about politics. It's about personality."*

Psychologist Allen Frances concluded his N.Y. Times article in 2017 like this: *"Psychiatric name-calling is a misguided way of countering Mr. Trump's attack on democracy. He can, and should, be appropriately denounced for his ignorance, incompetence, impulsivity, and pursuit of dictatorial powers."*[102]

350 health professionals. In the same year (2019), Congress received a warning letter signed by 350 health professionals claiming Trump's mental health is deteri-orating dangerously amid impeachment proceedings. With formulations like *"as the time of possible impeachment approaches, Donald Trump has the real potential to become ever more dangerous, a threat to the safety of our nation."* [103]

Dr. Todd Grande discussed Donald Trump's observ-able behavior *"in the context of narcissism"* based on statements Trump has made and observable things he has done. *"Considering all the information available, there does seem to be a clear alignment between Trump's behavior and narcissism. ... the issue of narcissism seems pretty clear; the issue then becomes, is his narcissism adaptive or maladaptive? About Donald Trump, I don't believe it's a matter whether or not his narcissism is maladaptive; it almost certainly is."* This assertion was made in late 2020. [104]

Dr. Steven Hassan, a Moon cult member when he was a college student, said he was brainwashed to the degree that he could have killed his parents if asked about it by the leaders. Dr. Hassan said in a 2022 interview that Trump has managed to create a cult using the same brainwashing methods as the Moon cult and the Jim Jones cult to create a MAGA cult within the MAGA movement. He opined that Trump has a malignant style of narcissistic behavior; he demands total obedience, which is the stereotypical profile of other cult leaders.[105]

Dr. Lee again sounded an alarm that year in a YouTube interview *("Dr. Bandy Lee about Trump's mental health:")*: *"Trump grew up in a mob-friendly, crime-friendly family. He experienced abandonment at the age of two and a half when his mother was hospitalized, and his father was too busy. His incapability to handle the pandemic and his attempted coup—all this was predictable based on his psychological structure."* [106]

In June 2023, **Leonard L. Glass, associate professor of psychiatry** at Harvard Medical School, wrote a letter to the editor of the New York Times: *"Donald Trump never apologizes, acknowledges a mistake, or appears to reflect on his role in the creation of his recurrent difficulties. As a practicing mental health professional for over 40 years, I believe that peo-*

ple can change, but I also know it is often difficult and painful work, sometimes requiring a therapist to help illuminate why one keeps finding oneself in the same kind of difficulty. This is the central problem that other mental health experts and I addressed in our 2017 book "The Dangerous Case of Donald Trump" and is what makes him unfit to hold high office. He has to be right, never needs to learn from his mistakes, and must protect his inflated and fragile self-image above all else, including the nation's security. He is always the victim, never having had a hand in the creation of his own dilemmas." [107]

Regardless of definitions, it is necessary to take a reality check:

We have all witnessed Trump's dangerous attempts to stay in power after his election loss in 2020. Some of these acts include his leading role in the Capitol insurrection in January 2021, his wild lies, and his threats toward anyone opposing him, whether politically or legally. The list grows longer each day.

Americans are facing an awkward 2024 presidential election. Two rather old candidates show possible signs of cognitive decline, and one is a convicted criminal. (May 31, 2024, Trump found guilty of 34 felony counts by a Manhattan jury in the "Hush "money/falsifying documents case.) Both are older than any president before. The situation could have been better, considering the presidential term is another four years...

Is the presidential election of 2024 in for some last-minute surprises? Could Republican Nikki Haley or Democrats Kamala Harris or Gavin Newsom become contenders before the finish line?

James Gilligan said back in 2017: *"The real challenge with Trump is not to define his mental state of health but to understand, react, and cope with the consequences of his behavior."* This observation seems even more relevant with each passing day: The issue is not whether Trump has a mental illness. It is whether he is dangerous.

A STARK WARNING:

*"…for those of us who have followed Trump's career from the start, the worldview he has trotted out to the public is no surprise. Some people seem shocked that he embraces torture without compunction, openly admires the suppression of freedom by Chinese and Russian dictators, and shows little grasp of ethics, governance, or constitutionalism, as evidenced by his insistence that the U.S. openly engage in war crimes (by killing the families of terrorists). He often seems ignorant of history and the economic benefits of free trade, dismissing the U.S. alliance and trading system that won the Cold War as "obsolete," regularly calling for punitive tariffs and insisting over and over again, "We never win any more," as if trade were a zero-sum game (which it is not). He relishes the idea that people at his rallies punch each other, suggesting that his supporters "knock the crap out of" any disrupters. But, as a Trump biographer, I can tell you these views fundamentally define the man. And **if you're looking—or perhaps hoping—for something more, you shouldn't expect to find it.** If you are seeking reassurance that the man who could be the next president of the United States possesses a coherent political philosophy or ethical foundation other than this rather pre-En-*

lightenment code of behavior—that he subscribes to the ideals of the Founders or has studied and understood American democracy, human rights, and our Constitutional system—you won't get it." From D'Antonio's book "Never Enough, Donald Trump and the Pursuit of Success."[108]

CHAPTER 7

TRUMP'S ADMIRATION FOR DICTATORS AND AUTHORITARIAN LEADERS

About Vladimir Putin, Russia's President from 2008 until now, and, in reality, a dictator since around 2010:

Trump won the 2016 presidential election with possibly help from Russian influence on social media. (Russia's goal, as determined by the U.S. intelligence community, backed up by evidence from the Special Counsel Robert Mueller report: Damage the Clinton campaign, boost Trump's chances, and sow distrust in American democracy.) [109]

Not surprisingly, Trump must have been, and is very thankful to Putin. Several incidents show how he is not only thankful but also admires Putin, seeing him as the leader he aspires to be. Trump telling Fox News host Bill O'Reilly (2015) that Putin gets an 'A' for leadership is quite a telling example. At an international summit in Helsinki in 2018, standing side by side with Putin, he said he was taking the word of Putin over his own director of national intelligence! An example of par excellence of political naivety.

In Europe, we know the realities of Putin's iron-hand regime closely. He became Prime Minister in 1999, a two-term President from 2000-2008, Prime Minister from 2008-2012 (two terms was the maximum for a president, so he was elegantly *"elected"* to be Prime Minister from 2008-2012—and resumed his presidency in 2012, re-*"elected"* in 2018 and finally (?) in March 2024 again was *"elected"* to another 6-year term as President.[110]His regime gradually evolved from autocracy to dictatorship, where political opposition is no longer tolerated.[111]

The Putin-regime quickly expedites voices of opposition by imprisoning, poisoning, or sudden *"accidents"* like falling from the 5th floor, etc.[112]

Opposition politician Vladimir Kara-Murza, 42, was jailed last April for 24 years, the harshest sentence so far for speaking out against the war. He was charged with *"treason"* after using a speech in the United States to say Russia had committed "war crimes" against Ukraine. He is now in a remote prison, reported to have serious health problems.

According to CPJ, Committee to Protect Journalists, thirteen journalists have been killed in contract-style murders since Russian President Vladimir Putin took office. No one has been brought to justice in any of the slayings.

Trump, Dec 20, 2015: *"...in all fairness to Putin, you're saying he killed people. I haven't seen that. I don't know that he has. Have you been able to prove that? Do you know the names of the reporters that he's killed?*

The last victim in a row of opposition voices killed by the regime so far was Alex Navalny, who *"suddenly died when going for a walk"* in a remote prison camp. (February 2024).

There are, as of today, no national political figures that can openly criticize Putin any longer. All opposition is effectively muted.

Putin has invaded neighboring countries three times since 2010, with only weak international reactions to the first two:

- Georgia in 2008: A full-scale land, air, and sea invasion, including its undisputed territory, on August 8, referred to as a *"peace enforcement."*
- Crimea, part of Ukraine in 2014: This invasion elicited a little international reaction.
- The rest of Ukraine in February 2022: A full-scale land, air, and sea invasion, named a *"special operation"* to conduct *"peacekeeping"* operations there.

Trump's response to the latter? He praised Russian President Vladimir Putin's moves in Ukraine, calling him *"savvy"* and saying, *"This is genius."*

Maybe it's not so strange that Putin would be more than happy to have Trump for another four years. Recently, Putin has declared that he would prefer Biden as president—in reality a cunning move to conceal from the public his natural choice, Trump, for whom Russia supposedly will work actively in 2024, as they did in the 2016 election.

About Kim Jong Un, North Korea:

"He leads 1.4 billion people, and there is no doubt who the boss is." Trump had a one-year *"affair"* with Kim Jong Un in 2018/2019, with meetings and 27 letters exchanged between them, which Trump described as *"beautiful."* [113] After a year of negotiating, the contacts were broken off, and nothing much has happened since then. However, it seemed they got along well, and Trump claims to have kept in contact with Kim Jong Un after he left the presidency. From the 27-letter correspondence, Kim Jong Un showed a positive attitude toward possible international detente. But in the end, it met with almost unilateral requests from the U.S., which seemed to be the main reason the negotiations were stranded.

However likable Kim Jong Un seems to be, it cannot hide that he is, as Trump said, *"the boss,"* whose dictatorial power is unlimited. Many years of dictatorship, first by his grandfather, Kim Il Sung, then his father, Kim Jong Il, and since 2011, his son Kim Jong Un, have led the country to become one of the poorest in the world, both economically and regarding human rights. It is a totalitarian system, rigidly state-controlled and dependent on a cult of personality.

North Korea is just another example of how dictatorial power leads to a life of luxury for the few and a harsh life with few rights for the many.

About Xi Jinping, Chairman of the Communist Party, China:

When the President and Leader of the Communist Party in China, Xi Jinping, managed to consolidate his power by eliminating the time limit for how long he could stay in power, Trump said: ***"He is now President for life.*** *President for life! And he is great! I think it is wonderful.* ***Maybe we should try it here one day."***

"He runs 1.4 billion people with an iron fist. Smart, brilliant, everything perfect." (My simple comment: *"Mr. Trump, did you forget the people under his iron fist?"*)

However intelligent, strong, and wonderful Xi Jinping may be (and his Communist Party predecessors might have been), it is difficult to overlook that the population suffers under harsh limitations of freedom, with their fate in the hands of the Party and its leaders.

China is a country that will dominate the world scene politically and economically in the years to come. There is no doubt about that. But will its citizens be able to benefit from this? Economically, to a certain extent—but as long as the rigid internal one-party system exists, there will continue to be a small Party-national and Party-local elite who reap most of the benefits and freedom of speech.

About Viktor Orban, the authoritarian leader of Hungary:

Viktor Orban has been Hungary's prime minister and *"strongman"* since 2010. He is yet another leader who has slowly but surely managed to seize almost total political power in Hungary, transforming the country from a democracy into an autocracy by:

- Controlling the nationwide right-wing media network,
- Gerrymandering local districts to get votes in his favor, and
- Staffing the public prosecutor's office with loyalists, *"ensuring that any misconduct by those in power stays hidden."* says Gabor Scheiring (Member of the Hungarian Parliament from 2010 to 2014.).[114]

Under his leadership, Hungary became the first non-democracy in the European Union. That does not bother Donald Trump, who recently said, *"You're respected all over Europe. Probably, like me, a little bit controversial, but that's OK,"* *"You've done a good job. You've kept your country safe."* (My editorial note: Orban is NOT respected all over Europe. He is the *"enfant terrible"* in the European Union, partly because of his domestic policy and *"serious and persistent breaches of EU values,"* [115]including violation of human rights and ongoing violations of rule of law principles[116], partly because he for a long time blocked Sweden's and Finland's NATO membership.)

Donald Trump's assessment: *"One of the strongest leaders anywhere in the world.*

CHAPTER 8

TRUMP'S INCESSANT LIES, LIES, LIES

"Everyone is entitled to his own opinion,
but not to his own facts."
—Daniel Patrick Moynihan.

Politicians do not have a good reputation for being truthful. Of course, there are exceptions, but the fact is that it is rare to find politicians who do not at least stretch the facts.

However, Donald Trump's problem is that he lies so much that Al Pacino's quote seems fitting: *"I always tell the truth, even when I lie."*

An abundance of lies and misleading statements compared to other politicians.

Trump's lying has reached such levels that it is fair to say he is outclassing any other current U.S. politician in the art of deception. The biggest and most significant of Trump's many (documented) lies is, of course, the *"Big Election Lie"*—the claim that *"the election was stolen from me, the election was rigged."* As **Ruth Ben-Ghiat, historian and author**, shrewdly observes: *"…psychologically, the "big lie" was very important because it prevented his propagandized followers from having to reckon with the fact that he lost."*[117]

The Washington Post has fact-checked everything Trump has said since the first day of his presidency and found, as of January 2019, over 8,158 untrue or misleading statements.[118] (But other presidents are not entirely free of lies; former President Obama made *"only"* 71 false claims throughout his eight years as president.) So, for most, or perhaps all presidents and politicians, take their claims with a grain of salt. However, Trump seems to be an extreme case regarding consistent lying. It could be tempting, in his case, to assume that everything he claims is a lie to be on the safe side.

A selection of Donald Trump's lies.

Let's look at some examples showing that Trump, unfortunately, cannot stop lying:

- Trump: *"We have a president (Joe Biden) that has no respect from the world."*

Fact check by Pew Research Center, June 2021: All 12 countries surveyed (Western Europe, Australia, Canada, Japan, and South Korea, but not Russia and China) showed significantly higher trust in Biden than in Trump.

Confidence in Trump ranged between 9% and 25%, while confidence in Biden ranged between 67% and 85%.

- Trump: *"Windmills are the most expensive energy in the world."*

Fact check: The U.S. Department of Energy reported in 2023 that windmills continue to be one of the lowest-cost sources of electricity in America.

- Trump: *"Biden's decision to withdraw from Afghanistan left $85 billion of equipment."*

Fact check: In 2022, the Pentagon reported the amount of equipment lost was $7 billion. (This is still a considerable loss, but $85 billion is vastly out of proportion with the facts.)

- Trump: *"Wisconsin has essentially admitted that I won (referring to the 2020 presidential election). I won the election up there."*

Fact check: The number of votes in Biden's favor was narrow but precise: 1,630,866 votes against Trump's 1,610,184 votes. Trump's campaign paid $3 million for a recount in two *"suspicious"* counties. The recount showed a net gain of 87 votes for Biden compared to the original count.

- Donald Trump repeatedly claimed he graduated *"first in his class."*

This is a documented falsehood; his grades have never been revealed, and he never appeared on the university's honor rolls.

And from one of the recent court proceedings, after a D.C. grand jury in August 2023 voted to indict Donald Trump in connection with the January 6 attack on the U.S. Capitol:

- Trump: *"This was a Biden administration against him."* Reality: Career officials from multiple agencies acted according to standard procedures to perform their duties. Prosecutor Jack Smith had to clarify in writing: *"It is necessary to set the record straight on the underlying facts that led to this prosecution because the defendants (Trump and his team) paint an inaccurate and distorted picture of the events. The defendants' misstatements, if unanswered, leave a highly misleading impression on a number of matters… The defendants rely on a pervasively false narrative of the investigation's origins. The defendants' insinuations should not stand uncorrected."*

Let me round off this row of lies from Trump with some recent claims, all of which were decided false by PolitiFact.[119]

- January 11, 2024, in a campaign ad: *"Haley's plan cuts Social Security benefits for 82% of Americans."*
- In a statement to the media on February 16, 2024, *"President Joe Biden directed New York AG Witch Hunt into Donald Trump's real estate dealings."*

- In a speech on March 9, 2024, Trump stated: *"Biden has implemented a formal policy that grants illegal aliens who enter the United States immunity from deportation."*
- On the same day, at a Georgia rally: *"In February alone, nearly 1 million jobs held by native-born Americans disappeared."*

Robert Reich has gathered 40 of Trump's biggest broken promises, which are presented in a video on YouTube and Facebook. Reich's advice and warning to the media: *"Don't let Donald Trump's lies become 'near truths.' Report his lies as lies. It's as simple as that."* (From an interview with Lou Dobs at the Mike Lindell Pillow Channel.)[120]

But when you have a cult leader whose lies are not denounced by leading Republican officials, maybe not be a big surprise to hear like this from MAGA cult members: *"He (Trump) never lied to the American people. He always told us the truth."* Another woman added, *"I know it in my heart. I know it in my spirit. He (Trump) has never lied about anything."* (A female Trump fan to an interviewer.)

Ponzi mindset?

I recently saw a documentary [121] about Charles Ponzi—the man infamously known for the "Ponzi scheme"—and the similarity between Ponzi's and Trump's minds struck me. Both men are delusional about some realities but have a never-give-up attitude and creative, persistent, and cynical business ideas, with no concern for whether pursuing their goals could cause significant harm to others. It is also fascinating to see how they both believed so much in their ideas that they made promises and lied excessively without blinking an eye—Ponzi, that he would one day be able to pay his rapidly growing massive debt that far exceeded his income streams, and Trump, that the presidential election was stolen from him and that he would one day be president again.

Ponzi was caught by people who were losing faith in him, leading to his quick economic ruin, and by the law, which caught up with his fraud. He was sentenced to five years in prison for federal crimes and, four years later, was found guilty and sentenced to seven more years in jail as a notorious thief.

Trump is on the verge of a similar destiny. People are losing faith in him, and now, in 2024, he faces lawsuits for criminal and civil offenses.

After Ponzi had served his time in prison, he was deported to Italy. He eventually ended up in Brazil, divorced, and ran a rooming house until he died in 1949 in a charity ward. Just before his death, he allegedly confessed to a reporter that his business had been simple: The old scheme of "robbing Peter to pay Paul."

Let's talk about truth for a second.

Is telling the truth really true? Well, yes and no—it depends. Astrophysicist Neil deGrasse Tyson clarifies that "telling the truth" may be true—or maybe not. In the holder's view, it could simply be a belief regarded as the truth. He says:

"There are three kinds of truth: Objective, Personal, and Political truths."[122]

- Personal *"truths"*: Not a verifiable truth, but a belief you hold dearly, based on your perception. *"The rivers, mountains, and streams are a spirit energy God manifests in nature." "Jesus is my savior."* Then you have suicide bombers who blow themselves up in a crowd, killing infidels, believe they will be reunited with Allah; this is another example of a personal belief that the person holds as *"truth."*

- Political *"truths"*: Beliefs that have become true because of your background, politically or culturally, and have been incessantly repeated as truths. And then you believe it to be true. Trump's election lie can serve as an excellent example: *"The 2020 presidential election was stolen from me by voter fraud."* This is a typical political "truth"—for those who believe in it.

  The problem with personal and political *"truths"* is that they are beliefs, not verifiable truths or facts—and not everyone believes in them. They are disputable and subject to individual differences, culture, and cognitive biases. You can't convince someone else about these *"truths"* without persuasion, constant repetition, or, at the limit, an act of violence.

- Objective truths: Whether you believe it or not, it is true. No matter who you are, what you believe in, where you live, or how old you are, an objective truth transcends all that. 1+1 is 2 in the morning, in the afternoon, at any time. Jump off a tall building, and gravity will smash you into the ground—no matter what *"higher power"* you worship. The attack on Congress on January 6, 2021, was documented by facts; it was not *"a peaceful demonstration."*

Tyson wisely remarks that national leaders who distance themselves from objective truths and rely on their own political views are *"a recipe for the unraveling of an informed democracy."*

I couldn't agree more when I observed how Trump and his collaborators are directly or indirectly, but very obviously, denying objective, fact-based truths. I guess that Trump's truth claims are coming close to the kind of truthiness, as defined by TV satirist Stephen Colbert—"truth that comes from the gut rather than facts."

Does Donald Trump believe his own lies?

Some of his lies, like the *"election stolen"* lie, are repeated so often—not only by himself but echoed throughout the MAGA base—that even if he did not believe it himself from the start, he may eventually have become a believer in his falsehood. Lying is a numbers game. The more it is repeated, the more people begin believing it, eventually catching up with the liar himself.

However, as a compulsive liar, he often lies without even considering whether it is true. Other times, he likely wants so much for the lies to be the truth that he begins to believe in them, at least some of them—such as the election lie mentioned above.

Lies as a means to get an advantage.

There are many examples of how Trump cynically uses a lie as long as it gives him an advantage. Former Vice President Pence recounts a conversation he had with Trump, published in the Wall Street Journal:

"Texas Rep. Louie Gohmert and other Republicans had filed a lawsuit asking a federal judge to declare that I had 'exclusive authority and sole discretion' to decide which electoral votes should count. 'I don't want to see "Pence Opposes Gohmert Suit" as a headline this morning,' the president said. I told him I did oppose it. 'If it gives you the power,' he asked, 'why would you oppose it?'"

What the Bible says about lying:

The Bible uses strong language regarding God's stance on lying. From Psalm 34:12-13: *"Whoever of you loves life and desires to see many good days, keep your tongue from evil and your lips from speaking lies."* Proverbs 6:16-10 says, *"There are six things that the Lord hates, seven that are an abomination to him: ... a lying tongue and one who sows discord among brothers."* The Bible language is black and white about lying, which is mentioned numerous times throughout its texts. So, there seems to be little wiggle room to debate how God feels about lying... Not to forget that lying is condemned by all central religious beliefs, whether Christianity, Buddhism, Hinduism, Judaism, or

Islam. Probably also (my guess, though!) by all or most of the 4,000 registered religions today.[123]

So, it is a bit strange that Donald Trump, a notorious liar, has recently (spring 2024) started a side career as a Bible seller (complementing his recent promotions of the $99 perfume *"for the movers, the shakers, and the history makers,"* and his gold-plated *"Never Surrender"* sneakers). His message now: *"Help us spread the Christian values."* This is from a man who, when asked about his favorite Bible verses, responded, *"I don't want to talk about it."* When asked, *"Do you ever ask for forgiveness, do you ever pray?"* he answered, *"Not really."*

The reason for suddenly promoting the Bible seems obvious: to make money and attract Christians. He now has to pay legal fees in his court cases, including one where, in 2016, he spent "hush money" to a porn star to hide that he had sex with her while his wife was home with a newborn baby. If that story had gone public, he calculated it would reduce his chances of being elected president in 2016.

Trump cunningly promotes the Bible in concert with country singer Lee Greenwood, known for his beautiful song *"God Bless the U.S.A."* He impeccably packages the *"God Bless America"* Bible with excellent leather-like binding—even including The Constitution(!). Given his attempt to overturn the election, the whole package could easily be considered a masterpiece of hypocrisy. But considering the massive attention given to it by the media and Trump's large supporter base, I wouldn't be surprised if it becomes popular among MAGA supporters, helping to get more dollars to pay Trump's lawyers. I would not buy it, knowing where parts of the revenue stream go.

Let me round off with a couple of words of wisdom about lying:

> *"Things come apart so easily when they have been held together with lies."*
> —Dorothy Allison.

Let's wait and see.

CHAPTER 9

DONALD TRUMP—A FORMER PRESIDENT NOW ENTANGLED IN LAWSUITS[124]

> *"Mercy to the guilty is*
> *cruelty to the innocent."*
> —Adam Smith.

America is now witnessing a former president who is showing shocking disrespect for the authority of the law, using threats against those representing it and, in doing so, undermining trust in the judiciary system. With the help of money, powerful and influential friends, temporary immunity from civil offenses while president, and an army of lawyers, he has managed to delay many (but not all) civil and criminal charges.

The near future will reveal whether he eventually runs into the same problems as Mr. Gotti, a Mafia boss who acquired the nickname *"Teflon Don"* because, for years, he managed to escape several criminal convictions. But the law eventually caught up with Gotti. In 1992, he was imprisoned for life for criminal offenses.

Frankly, dealing with Trump's clashes with the law has been overwhelming, not only because of the staggering number of lawsuits but also because of the almost absurd situation in which a former president of the U.S.—and a possible candidate for the next presidency—has spent most of his adult life involved in various attempts to break or circumvent the law. The situation is neatly summed up in an article from February 2024 in The Atlantic:

"Not long ago, the idea that a former president—or major-party presidential nominee—would face serious legal jeopardy was nearly unthinkable. Today, merely keeping track of the many cases against Donald Trump requires a law degree, a great deal of attention, or both."[125] An updated tracking of Trump's ongoing court cases can be found here: [126]

By the way, that article *"only"* looks at the present court cases, not the past ones. Getting a broader picture of Donald Trump's previous law encounters is a task worthy of Sisyphus.[127] But the article *"Donald Trump: Three decades, 4,095 lawsuits" shows the vast scope., presented in a simplified graphic form."* [128]Complaints and charges were brought forward by various private and business plaintiffs, including numerous cases brought forward by Trump and his companies.

But let's move on to the present situation. Forgotten is *"The Art of the Deal."* Donald Trump and his legal team are now focusing exclusively on and enhancing *"The Art of Delaying, Disrupting, Deflecting, and Denying,"* supplemented by Trump's unhinged, dangerous, and demeaning threats that serve no legal purpose but increase tension every-where. He acts as if he is invincible but has recently lost a civil case in New York, received a pair of significant def-amation judgments, and found guilty of criminal offenses in the recent "hush money" case. He has already stated he will appeal.

As of mid-2024, Trump now faces 91 felony counts across two state courts and two different federal districts, risking a prison sentence in any of them.

Meanwhile, he is the leading Republican candidate in the race to become the next president. The timeline for these cases has now become not only a legal battle but a race against time, as it is clear that he intends to *"kill"* the cases if he is elected.

The 3 D's: Deny, Delay, Distract.

Throughout all the civil and criminal court cases Trump has been involved in, there is a crystal-clear pat-tern: deny, delay, and distract. He tries to obstruct any investigation about him or his company. This strategy has been ongoing for decades, enthusiastically and successfully pushed by Donald Trump and his lawyers. The one taking the *"honor"* of teaching Trump this tactic is the infamous attorney Roy Cohn, alias *"the fixer"* for the mob. He met Donald Trump (and his father, Fred) for the first time in 1973 when their company was facing allegations from the government for not letting Black people rent their apartments in Brooklyn. Roy Cohn advised, *"Just go on the offensive, don't admit guilt, do not back down."* Roy Cohn became Donald Trump's mentor for 13 years and taught

131

him the key strategies when facing allegations: denial, delay, and distraction. This strategy has become Trump's *"trademark"* when facing allegations.

However, there are signs that this tactic might not be effective in the long run. Civil and criminal charges are piling up; some have already been lost (the Trump University case the "hush money case" where he received a criminal conviction, and the E. Carroll defamation case), and others await court trials after grand juries unanimously found enough evidence to indict.

Trump's legal downward path.

October 2016: Trump University scam case.

This might have been the first signs of Trump's legal downward path.

After three separate lawsuits were filed from 2010 to 2013, Donald Trump agreed in late 2016 to pay the students $25 million in settlement. The CAP20 investigative report concluded in early 2017: "If the affairs of Trump University are any indication, then Trump has proven himself to be quite comfortable exploiting the hopes, dreams, and fears of vulnerable Americans." [129]

Soon after his presidential term from 2016 to 2020, more legal cases were lost:

May 2022: Donald Trump was fined for contempt of court by ignoring a subpoena to hand in documents.

A member of the New York attorney general's office stated that Trump did not hand over *"even a single responsive document"* in response to a subpoena in December. He eventually submitted the required documents in May 2022 and paid a $110,000 fine.

August 2022: Civil lawsuits from Capitol police officers for causing their injuries were filed in by 11 officers.

Hundreds of Capitol Police officers claim they have been traumatized by the violence at the Capitol, and eleven Police officers have filed civil lawsuits against him, seeking compensation for physical and emotional injuries inflicted upon them during the battle scenes outside the Congress on January 6, 2021. [130]

Trump and his lawyers claim immunity for these cases, arguing that as a former president, he cannot face civil lawsuits resulting from his role in the January 6 attack. (Why is Trump scared of these lawsuits? According to him, no violence occurred on January 6, claiming his supporters were *"hugging and kissing police…"*)

The U.S. Court of Appeals for the District of Columbia Circuit ruled in November 2023 that the lawsuits could proceed, stating he was not acting as a president but *"in his personal capacity as a presidential candidate." "Today's ruling makes clear that those who endanger our democracy and the lives of those sworn to defend it will be held to account,"* Patrick Malone, a lawyer for the officers, said in a statement. However, Trump has appealed to the Supreme

Court, and that case has yet to be finally decided as of May 2024.[131]

December 2022: The Trump organization was found guilty of the tax fraud scheme.

A 12-person jury found Trump Corp. and Trump Payroll Corp. guilty of seventeen felonies, including criminal tax fraud and falsifying business records. Among the charges was hiding compensation given to top executives. The scam had been going on for 13 years. The organization was fined $1.6 million, the maximum penalty allowed by law. Donald Trump himself denied any wrongdoing, but his Chief Financial Officer, Allen Weisselberg, was sentenced to—and later served—five months in jail.

2019–May 2024: The E. Carroll sexual abuse and defamation civil case. Donald Trump was found guilty by the Manhattan court jury.

The verdict about sexual harassment is final. The amount to pay for defamation has been appealed and is awaiting a decision.

The case was originally opened in 2019 (while Trump was still President) when author E. Jean Carroll filed a defamation lawsuit with the New York Supreme Court, stating that Trump had damaged her reputation, substantially harmed her professionally, and caused emotional pain. She explained the case in an email to National Public Radio: *"Decades ago, the now President of the United States raped me. When I had the courage to speak out about the attack, he defamed my character, accused me of lying for personal gain, and even insulted my appearance. No woman should have to face this. But this lawsuit is not only about me. I am filing this on behalf of every woman who has ever been harassed, assaulted, silenced, or spoken up, only to be shamed, fired, ridiculed, and belittled."*

The case was drawn out, starting with Donald Trump's complete denial, "*She is not even my type,*" followed up by government lawyers from the Department of Justice (DOJ) asserting that Trump had acted in his official capacity. Carroll's lawyer, Roberta Kaplan, responded by saying, *"Trump's effort to wield the power of the U.S. government to evade responsibility for his private misconduct is without precedent."*The case was moved on by the DOJ, claiming that Trump was shielded by his former office as U.S. president.

In November 2022, Carroll made a renewed claim of defamation, referring to Trump's statements on Truth Social from October. In this second suit, it was alleged that Trump manhandled Carroll, "*pulled down her tights," groped around her genitals and raped her."*

After more battling back and forth, essentially initiated by Trump's lawyer team to further delay the court trial, proceedings finally started on April 25, 2023.

An anonymous jury of six men and three women was appointed. Anonymous to both parties, the lawyers involved in the case, and even to the judge.

The anonymity of jurors is seldom used; according to Reporters Committee for Freedom of the Press, these are criteria that can be used to determine if an anonymous jury is appropriate: The defendant's involvement in organized crime, the defendant's participation in a group with the capacity to harm jurors, the defendant's past attempts to interfere with the judicial process, the potential that the defendant will get a long jail sentence or substantial fines if convicted, and extensive publicity that could expose jurors to intimidation or harassment. Used in cases about drug cartels, mafia bosses, and other trials where the safety of the jurors is very likely to be in danger.

The reason for protecting the jury in this case was Trump's dangerous rhetoric against officials during the Stormy Daniels hush money case.

Verdict: On May 9, after hearing the testimonies and evidence, the jury found Donald Trump guilty of sexual harassment and defamation of the plaintiff, E. Jean Carroll. Initially, a unanimous jury sentenced him to pay $5 million in damages. However, after Trump continued his defamatory statements, another unanimous jury in January 2024 increased the amount to $83.3 million.

Trump has appealed to reduce the amount, although the verdict on sexual harassment is final and cannot be appealed.

Carroll stated that her life was completely changed for the worse when then-President Donald Trump publicly claimed her allegations of sexual abuse were fabricated, adding that she was not his type. She now sleeps with a gun at her bedside due to the dozens of nasty, insulting, and sometimes outright threatening tweets and messages she receives daily, making her fear for her life. Carroll also claims that her professional life has been negatively impacted. Her lawsuit sought both punitive and compensatory damages.

2018–May 2024: The Manhattan criminal *"hush money case."* **The first criminal trial of a former US president in history. Trump was found guilty on 34 felony counts.**

In March 2023, a New York grand jury indicted Trump on 34 felony charges for allegedly falsifying business records to cover up hush money payments to women who claimed they had sexual encounters with him. After two granted delays, Judge Juan Merchan refused further postponements, and the trial began on April 15, 2024, more than a year after the charges were brought. On May 31, 2024, a 12-person jury unanimously found Donald Trump guilty on all 34 felony counts.

Politically Motivated?

I noticed an interview with three Trump supporters on April 15, the start day of the trial, who said they came to show their support, claiming the case was old and brought up now only for political reasons. The facts, however, tell a different story. The first investigations in the case started in 2017 but were closed in 2019 for unknown reasons. The case reopened in 2021.

Cyrus Vance revealed the answer in a *"Meet the Press"* interview when asked by Chuck Todd:

"Why didn't you charge the hush money case? Why didn't you ever charge it in 2018, 2019, or 2020?" Vance replied, *"I was asked by the U.S. Attorney's Office of the Southern District to stand down on our investigation, which had commenced involving the Trump Organization. And as you know, as someone who*

respects that office a great deal and believes that they may have perhaps the best laws to investigate, I did so.

… I was surprised, after Michael Cohen pleaded guilty, that the investigation from the Southern District on that issue did not go forward."

In other words, the Department of Justice in the Trump administration intervened, which is why the case did not come up until later when it was "free" from DOJ pressure.

Many people have compared this criminal case to Al Capone's conviction for tax evasion: It's not that Capone didn't deserve the verdict of 11 years imprisonment, but his gangster reputation was based on other crimes. This charge against Trump for an alleged criminal offense might, in the same way, seem minor compared to his even more sinister cases, like attacking elections or putting national secrets at risk.

Each of these six cases ended in legal losses. This was just an overture to what was coming: Four more court cases are unfolding but still awaiting court trials. Let's take a closer look:

June 2023—: The *"Mar-a-Lago Documents"* case. Prosecuted by the Department of Justice for illegally removing confidential documents from the White House. Charges include possible violation of the Espionage Act.

The case in a nutshell: Trump took boxes of classified documents to his private property (Mar-a-Lago), where they were stored haphazardly. The indictment focuses on his refusal to return them to the government despite repeated requests.

When the case appeared public, Trump reacted in an interview with Sean Hannity on Fox News on September 22, 2022: "*If you are the President of the United States, you can declassify just by saying it's declassified, even by thinking about it.*" [132]

Did this sound like the words of a defiant young boy or a former president of the United States?

The charges, filed in June 2023 by special counsel Jack Smith, are severe: Trump is charged with 37 criminal felonies, including the deliberate retention of national security information and obstruction of justice (he did not respond to several requests from the FBI to return the documents). Not only did Trump put these documents at risk, but he also lied to the government through his lawyers, asserting they did not have these documents.

In a speech following his arraignment, Trump commented on the 37 federal charges he faces regarding the classified documents kept at Mar-a-Lago:

"Today, we witnessed the most heinous abuse of power in the history of our country. A corrupt sitting president had his top political opponent arrested for fake and fabricated charges for which he and numerous other presidents would be guilty. And when he is in the middle of a presidential election, in which he is losing badly. This is called election interference and yet another attempt to rig and steal another presidential election...."

But Trump's uninformed approach to handling critical classified documents had long been a concern among former employees. This case is, therefore, unsurprising for "insiders" who worked with Donald Trump in the White House. According to White House staffer Miles Taylor, "It appeared as though Trump believed the law did not apply to him... We were afraid to bring classified documents to Trump."

In one interview with Fox News, Donald Trump claimed he could declassify documents merely by thinking about them(!) This statement doesn't serve as a valid excuse but highlights Trump's profound misunderstanding of how national security should be handled.

While it may not be fitting to make light of such a severe issue, I couldn't help but smile when Jimmy Kimmel joked on his Live Show on March 3, 2022. He quipped: "They have so much evidence that Donald Trump tried to flush himself down the toilet this morning." He was, of course, referring to stories from Trump's staff that Trump, on several occasions, flushed important documents down the toilet, thereby violating the Presidential Records Act.[133]

It's worth noting that Trump is not the only U.S. president accused of breaking the Presidential Records Act. Bush, Clinton, Obama and Biden have all faced investigations regarding this issue.

But there are significant differences between Trump's actions and those of his predecessors—beyond that he reportedly violated this act multiple times during his presidency:

- The sheer volume of documents involved in the Mar-a-Lago case.
- The inclusion of classified documents within these piles.
- The blatant carelessness, allowing nearly "anyone" access.
- The refusal to return the documents—which ultimately forced the authorities to issue a subpoena.

The evidence is mounting, but Trump relentlessly has denied any responsibility, with posts like: "I AM AN INNOCENT MAN."

Judge Aileen Cannon, a Trump-appointed judge who is presiding over the case, has so far, in very creative but judicially doubtful ways, made progress in the case difficult. These moves have been welcomed in the Trump world but harshly criticized by reputable lawyers, saying her impartiality in favor of Trump is questionable. Some even accused her of "sabotaging" the case[134]

Trump's colossal efforts to delay everything are in the hope that if he gets elected president later this year, he will have the possibility of instructing the Department of Justice to dismiss the Department's cases against him—this one and the charges for inciting an insurrection.

Former federal prosecutor Glenn Kirchner expressed what I think is a widespread opinion: When the People vote in November, they should know if Donald Trump is guilty—or not guilty—of violating America's Espionage laws.[135]

October 2023-January 2024: The New York financial civil fraud case. The private Trump organization owned by Donald Trump was found guilty of overestimating property values to gain substantial economic advantages and *"unfair"* advantages in acquiring new businesses.

The verdict:

- A $355 million (plus interest) penalty for issuing false financial statements and business records over many years. Reports indicate there was *"copious evidence of financial fraud."*
- An independent monitor must supervise the Trump Organization for at least three years.

How was this fine calculated?

- $168 million in reduced loan interest, made possible by overstating property values in statements presented to banks, insurance companies, and other businesses.
- $126 million in *"ill-gotten"* profits from selling the old Post Office in Washington, D.C.
- $60 million in taxes due from the sale of Ferry Point in the Bronx.
- The fraud also enabled the Trump organization to acquire and develop hotels, golf courses, and other businesses that otherwise would not have been possible. This was not included in the fine but was

noted by the judge as additional benefits obtained through fraudulent financial statements.

Donald Trump could not secure either the total amount or bonds. According to his attorneys, securing bonds was a *"practical impossibility"* after being turned down by 30 surety companies. The appeals court subsequently reduced the sum to $175 million, which he managed to pay, temporarily putting the $464 million judgment against the former president and his associates on hold. The schedule for when the Appeals Court will decide on Trump's appeal is not yet set.

(I recently heard finance billionaire O'Leary comment that the business practices of Trump's organization are not unusual, with New York real estate developers now asking, *"Who's next?"* To Mr. O'Leary: There is a simple answer to who's next: Those who fraudulently manipulate their property values to unduly obtain advantages compared to businesses that operate ethically and adhere to legally accepted business practices.)

August 2023—: The Election Subversion case (trying to overturn the results of the 2020 election.) Prosecuted by the Department of Justice and indicted by a grand jury.

Donald Trump faces serious criminal charges. Here's an overview of the case: In August 2023, a D.C. grand jury indicted him for his attempts to undermine the 2020 presidential election. He is accused of deliberately spreading false fraud allegations, orchestrating bogus slates of electors, and trying to prevent the certification of the election results on January 6. According to the prosecutors, Trump targeted the *"bedrock function of the United States federal government: the nation's process of collecting, counting, and certifying the results of the presidential election."*

Specifically, the charges are:[136]

- Pressuring officials to violate their duty by coercing acting Attorney General Jeffrey Rosen and others in the Justice Department to endorse false claims of election fraud.
- Corruptly impeding an official proceeding, including a phone call that pressured Georgia Secretary of State Brad Raffensperger and the organization of fake elector teams.
- Conspiring to defraud the U.S. by aiding and comforting insurrectionists through inaction and inflammatory tweets about Vice President Pence.
- Assisting an insurrection.
- Inciting the overturning of a fair election and the government.
- Engaging in seditious conspiracy.

These allegations stem from detailed investigations, hundreds of witness testimonies, and the work of the Justice Department and the January 6 Committee. In October 2022, the Committee directly subpoenaed Trump, stating: *"You were at the center of the first and only effort by any US president to overturn an election and obstruct the peaceful transfer of power. The evidence demonstrates that you knew this activ-*

ity was illegal." Trump, however, did not comply with the subpoena.

Trump was indicted on August 1, 2023, with the court proceedings initially set for March 2024. However, the trial has faced delays.

August 2023—: The Georgia election interference case. Crimes to the County of Fulton, Georgia. Prosecutor: Fulton County by District Attorney Fanni Willis.

After nearly two years of investigations, Donald Trump, along with 19 others, including his White House Chief of Staff Mark Meadows, former New York City Mayor Rudy Giuliani, three of his lawyers, and his campaign leader, were indicted in Fulton County in August 2023. They face 13 felony counts related to a *"criminal enterprise"* aimed at maintaining Trump's power by attempting to overturn the 2020 election results in Georgia. This case, due to the number of people involved, is complex and challenging to follow, yet it significantly illustrates the extent of the attack on American democracy.

Here are some of the charges laid out by Fulton District Attorney Fanni Willis and confirmed by a grand jury:

- Violating Georgia's Racketeer Influenced and Corrupt Organizations Act (RICO).
- Attempting to coerce a public official, specifically the infamous request to Georgia's Republican Secretary of State Brad Raffensperger, to *"find"* 11,780 votes.

- Harassing an election worker by baselessly accusing her of fraud.
- Pressured Georgia lawmakers to disregard the voters' will and appoint a different slate of Electoral College electors favorable to Trump.
- Attempting unauthorized access to voting machines in a Georgia county and trying to steal data from the voting machine company.

The case has been complicated by the revelation of an ill-timed romantic relationship between Fanni Willis and Nathan Wade, an attorney she hired as a special prosecutor. This development added a *"soap opera"* element to the court proceedings, culminating in Wade's resignation.

Four co-defendants have pleaded guilty: Scott Hall and Trump lawyers Kenneth Cheseboro, Sidney Powell, and Jane Ellis. The trials for the remaining defendants are likely to occur in 2024.

This case is monumental, judicially and politically, and as with the DOJ's cases, time is of the essence. The Supreme Court faces a critical decision on whether Trump is immune from prosecution for acts committed while president or immediately after his term. If the Supreme Court rules in favor of immunity, it could significantly complicate, if not halt, this case.

In addition to this, Donald Trump faces more legal challenges in 2024. These proceedings are far from the only legal battles currently involving him:

Amendment 14, Section 3 in the Constitution: Is Donald Trump ineligible to serve again as president?

Expert lawyers, including Michael Luttig and Laurence Tribe, argue that Donald Trump is disqualified from holding office under Amendment 14, Section 3 of the U.S. Constitution, which states:

"No person shall be a Senator or Representative in Congress, or elector of President and Vice-President, or hold any office, civil or military under the United States, or under any State, who, having previously taken an oath... to support the Constitution of the United States, shall have engaged in insurrection or rebellion against the same, or given aid or comfort to the enemies thereof." Notably, this clause does not require a conviction.

These legal experts contend that Trump's efforts to overturn the 2020 election results and his incitement of the January 6 riot meet these criteria and, therefore, bar him from participating in the primaries. However, the Supreme Court has decided that states cannot remove any candidate from a presidential primary ballot without further action from Congress.

This case involved high stakes—not concerning a possible criminal conviction—but whether Trump meets the constitutional requirements to serve as president. Following this SCOTUS decision, Trump is set to appear on the ballot in every state.

Total immunity.—Can Donald Trump (or any president of the U.S.) commit any crime, including killing political enemies, without legal consequences?

Trump campaign spokesman Steven Cheung argued, *"Without complete immunity, a President of the United States would not be able to function properly!"* This assertion might sound absurd; it suggests a president could murder without ever being held accountable—something expected perhaps in authoritarian regimes like Russia or North Korea, but surely not in the United States. Yet, this is precisely the future Trump and his legal team seem to envision. It raises the question: is this what the majority of Americans want?

The U.S. District Court of D.C. dismissed his claim for presidential immunity. The judge emphatically stated, *"Defendant's four-year term as Commander-in-Chief did not endow him with the divine right of kings, exempt from the criminal accountability that governs his fellow citizens."* This decision underscores the critical role of the judiciary.

Nonetheless, the indefatigable and highly ambitious Donald Trump, supported by a team of lawyers beyond the reach of ordinary citizens, challenged this ruling and pushed for a hearing by the Supreme Court (SCOTUS). This puts SCOTUS in a precarious position, having to decide on a matter that will significantly affect the future of U.S. democracy: should they grant him immunity from any crimes if he is re-elected or uphold a democratic system with three independent branches of government, as most Americans would prefer?

As I write this, it's hard to believe what is unfolding. Can a court, even one perceived as politically biased, pave the way for autocracy or dictatorship? By agreeing to additional hearings, which are scheduled so late that the insurrection charges against Trump might not be addressed until after the November Presidential election, they have cracked open the door to such a possibility. Granting Trump a *"pass"* could be disastrous. It risks undermining the rule of law, diminishing the international credibility of the U.S., and easing the path for future coup attempts.

After seeing all these clashes with the law Donald Trump is and has been engaged in, let's have a look at the standard the strategy he and his lawyer teams have used and use.

Donald Trump's legal strategy is to claim immunity, plead "the fifth," deny, delay, attack judges, and try to undermine the courts' authority.

Donald Trump has, throughout these cases, consistently demonstrated denial—a typical reaction for many accused individuals—but his response has been notably aggressive and threatening. He verbally attacks legal representatives and adopts a victim stance, frequently claiming, *"This is a witch hunt."* This behavior aligns with what professionals recognize as a narcissistic pattern of:

Denial—Attack—Reverse Victim and Offender." [137]

Yet, the legal challenges continue accumulating for the former president, now an ordinary U.S. citizen, Mr. Donald Trump. It isn't very comfortable for someone who once led a great nation. His reactions have included:

- Claiming total immunity
- Pleading the Fifth Amendment
- Denying allegations
- Delaying proceedings
- Attacking judges and the courts for rulings he disagrees with, thereby creating mistrust in the judicial system. [138]

Immunity?

Trump asserted that he was immune from these lawsuits because his actions were part of his presidential duties. A Federal Judge blocked Trump's *"absolute immunity"* claim from the January 6 suits on February 18, 2022. The judge said his speech before the Capitol riot was *"the essence of a civil conspiracy"* and moved three civil suits against him forward.[139]

Additionally, on August 2, 2022, DC District Judge Amit Mehta dismissed Trump's immunity claim, noting that his actions on January 6 aimed to secure a second term. Thus, the lawsuits will proceed, though a trial date has yet to be set.

The Fifth.

"Say nothing because you might incriminate yourself." [140] Back in November 2014, Cosby was charged with sexual assault but remained silent in the court hearings. Then Trump tweeted: *"I am no fan of Bill Cosby, but nevertheless some free advice—if you are innocent, do not remain silent. You look guilty as hell!"*

And again in September 2017, Trump told a campaign crowd in Iowa: *"If you're innocent, why are you taking the Fifth Amendment?"*

He should know, as he has used The Fifth on several occasions himself, most likely to evade the truth:

In the divorce with Ivana in 1990, he invoked the fifth 97 times—mostly in response to questions about other women.

When had to appear on October 28, 2022, at the New York court civil inquiry (by Attorney General Letitia James) for alleged tax fraud? [141] He invoked the fifth 440 times!

I cannot resist comparing Mr. Trump with the Mafia boss Mr. Gotti, nicknamed *"Teflon Don."* Gotti was the head of the Gambino mafia family, known for his ability to evade several criminal charges against him over the years.

This nickname given to Gotti might also be a fitting nickname for Donald Trump.

The evasion road ended, though, for Mr. Gotti. In 1992, he was sentenced to life without parole.

Denials.

There are many examples of Trump's denials when confronted with charges of various natures, which Trump always denied. Some were settled, though, and some cases disappeared into thin air.

Delays.

Trump's various lawyer teams have become *"delay experts"* through their numerous defendant cases and court trials on behalf of Mr. Trump. A prime example is the legal case against Donald Trump, his three eldest children, and the Trump Organization. Attorney General Letitia James filed a civil lawsuit after "copious evidence of financial fraud" was found.

Trump's reaction? Attack and Delay.

So far, it seems he could have spared his rants: In February 2024, Trump was fined $355 million *"to ensure this fraud cannot continue,"* as Attorney General Letitia James said. Later, Trump was allowed to appeal after reaching an agreement to put up a bond of $175 million.

Experienced lawyers say the case might drag out for years, knowing Trump's money-backed twists and turns.[142]

Attack!

After his election defeat in 2020, Donald Trump has constantly been issuing threats against his perceived opponents, critics, and rivals. He often uses vague or inflammatory language to incite violence or intimidate others, especially those who pose a legal threat to him.

Trump's increasing use of threatening language is a stark warning sign. Some have described it as *"Poisoning the groundwater of democracy."* We are not talking about a few threats. They are flourishing. Trump has himself described them as *"Attacks on the Courts."* [143]

The big problem is that when threats are publicly made like that, some unhinged persons might take them as invitations. It is bad enough when said by some *"ordinary,"* not-so-well-known person, but it can be catastrophic when said by someone like Donald Trump, who is a national figurehead and has a cult-like supporter base.

The examples of Donald Trump's dangerous threats have become so numerous that this in itself is alarming. When directed against people representing the law, it not only creates dangers for the threatened persons but undermines the trust in the judiciary system—a dangerous step toward breaking down a democracy.

Trump's rants vary from general, like *"We stand up to those crooked democrat prosecutors all over the country..."* to direct death threats(!) When stating his agony toward the representatives of the law that dare to cross his path, he shockingly uses words like *"witch hunt," "crazy," "biased," "*anti-Trump," "Marxist," "fascist," "racist," and "subhuman"—even accusing some of crimes. Frankly, his statements have become like Hitler-like rage against perceived enemies and are repeated to the degree that many are becoming immune to his rhetoric and stop reacting. So far, he is quite successful in playing out the recipe for a wannabe autocrat who wants the law to align with his views and not be based on the rule of law.

I have compiled a list of insinuations and threats made by Donald Trump from 2020 onwards. However, I must credit Aaron Blake from the Washington Post, whose article *"A catalog of Trump's attacks on judges, prosecutors, and witnesses"* helped me make a reasonably complete list. [144]

Some of his statements are written in his *"Truth Social,"* and some are uttered in speeches or when talking with journalists. The threats and accusations are so many that I have listed the attacked persons in alphabetical order.

About U.S. District Court Judge Amy Berman Jackson.

In January 2020, Trump tweeted, *"There has rarely been a juror so tainted as the forewoman in the Roger Stone case. Look at her background. She never revealed her hatred of 'Trump' and Stone. She was biased, as was the judge. Roger wasn't even working on my campaign. Miscarriage of justice. Sad to watch!"*

After that, and until now (mid-2024), verbal attacks on prosecutors and judges have gradually intensified.

About Manhattan District Attorney Alvin Bragg, the first prosecutor to bring a criminal case against a current or former American president:

- "The Racist Manhattan District Attorney
- *"TRUMP HATING WIFE AND FRIENDS."*
- *"Soros-backed animal."*
- *"Prosecutorial Misconduct and Interference with an Election."*
- *"… degenerate psychopath."*
- *"The criminal is the district attorney because he illegally leaked massive amounts of grand jury information, for which he should be prosecuted."* (Trump did not provide evidence of this).
- *"Death and destruction"* if I'm indicted in New York.

Incredibly, he posted an image holding a baseball bat standing behind Bragg, seemingly getting ready to bash in Bragg's skull. Call it what you want. I call it a vile, dangerous act of inciting violence.

It was no surprise then that Bragg received an anonymous written death threat, which also contained a mysterious white powder. He was warned, *"ALVIN: I AM GOING TO KILL YOU,"* followed by 13 exclamation points.

About U.S. District Judge Tanya S. Chutkan, presiding over Trump's federal election fraud case:

- *"Oh, I'm sure she will be very fair"* (referring to an article claiming Chutkan's grandfather was a Marxist).
- *"She obviously wants me behind bars. VERY BIASED & UNFAIR!"*
- *"Highly partisan."*
- *"She admitted she's running election interference against Trump."* (She did not.)

Many felt threatened by his remarks, prompting Judge Chutkan to impose a gag order to restrict Trump from publicly attacking potential witnesses, prosecutors, and court personnel.

About Judge Arthur Engoron, who is both the judge and jury in Trump's civil business fraud case:

- *"A vicious, biased, and mean 'rubber stamp' for the Communist takeover of the great & prosperous American company that I have built over a long period of years."*
- *"Judge Arthur Engoron Is A Far-Left Democrat Who Said Trump Should Be Prosecuted Because 'He's Just A Bad Guy.'"*
- *"He's interfering with an election, and it's a disgrace."*
- (Judge Engoron is) *"...crooked."*

About Engoron's aide:

- *"[Sen. Charles] Schumer's girlfriend … is running this case against me."*

About New York Attorney General Letitia James, the prosecutor in Trump's civil business fraud case:

- *"We have a corrupted N.Y. Attorney General."* (Letitia James.)
- *"Another witch hunt by a racist attorney general."*
- *"This 'Monster…'"*
- *"What we have here is an attempt to hurt me in an election. This has to do with election interference, plain and simple."*
- *"Crazy, radical, leftist nutjob."*
- *"Deranged lunatic."*
- *"Likewise, Letitia James should resign for purposeful and criminal Election Interference."*
- *"James is 'corrupt,' and the case against me is 'ELECTION INTERFERENCE' and a politically motivated 'WITCH HUNT.'"*

In a direct threat, Trump used these exact words, comparable to a mafia boss statement:

- *"You ought to go after this attorney general."*

About Judge Lewis A. Kaplan, presiding over the sexual abuse and defamation E. Carroll case:

- *"This Clinton-appointed Judge, Lewis Kaplan, hated President Donald J. Trump more than is humanly possible."*

About Judge Juan Merchan, presiding over Trump's New York hush-money case:

- *"I have a Trump-hating judge with a Trump-hating wife and family whose daughter worked for Kamala Harris and now receives money from the Biden-Harris campaign."*
- *"The Judge 'assigned' to my Witch Hunt Case, a 'Case' that has NEVER BEEN CHARGED BEFORE, HATES ME."*

About Special Counsel Jack Smith, appointed to represent the government in the two criminal cases against Trump:

- *"A Trump Hater, as are all his friends and family."*
- *"He's a raging and uncontrolled Trump-hater, as is his wife."*
- *"Deranged Jack Smith has added a War Crimes Prosecutor from the Hague to his team … These Marxists and Fascists are killing our Country, and we're not going to let them get away with it."*
- *"A Radical Right Lunatic."*
- *"Psycho."*
- He *"probably 'planted' information in the 'boxes' given to them."* (There is no evidence of this.)
- *"Counselor Jack Smith is crooked and deranged."*

- *"Special Counsel, federal special prosecutor Jack Smith, and others should rot in Hell."*

About Fani Willis, District Attorney of Fulton County, Georgia, investigating Trump for his attempts to interfere with the state's election:

- *"They've got a local racist Democrat district attorney in Atlanta."*
- *"They say there's a young woman, a young racist in Atlanta, so racist…"*
- *"A family steeped in hate."* (citing her father as a Black Panther)[145]
- *"Right here in Georgia, you have a lunatic and Marxist district attorney of Atlanta…"*
- *"…rabid partisan."*
- (She is) *"out to 'get Trump.'"*
- *"Radical left"* prosecutor who was *"playing games with me."*

    Donald Trump does not stop there, claiming:

- *"Every time the radical left Democrats, Marxists, communists, and fascists indict me, I consider it a great badge of courage."*
- *"IF YOU GO AFTER ME, I'M COMING AFTER YOU!"*
- *"We stand up to those crooked Democrat prosecutors all over the country."*

These are just some examples of representatives of the law that Trump has verbally attacked since he lost the presidential election in 2020. *"Trump's attacks on judges poison the civil atmosphere and make physical attacks more likely,"* said retired Massachusetts judge and Harvard Law School lecturer Nancy Gertner. *"Trump is challenging the very role of judges."*

Sadly and dangerously, his rhetoric has not been limited to law enforcers but anyone perceived as opposing him. This has encouraged his supporters to commit numerous acts of violence, like the Capitol riot, the El Paso shooting, and countless other lesser-known incidents. ABC News found *"54 cases invoking 'Trump' in connection with violence, threats, alleged assaults." In at least 12 cases, perpetrators hailed Trump in the midst of, or immediately after, physically assaulting innocent victims. In another 18 cases, perpetrators cheered or defended Trump while taunting or threatening others. In another 18 cases, perpetrators cheered or defended Trump while taunting or threatening others. And in another 10 cases, Trump and his rhetoric were cited in court to explain a defendant's violent or threatening behavior."* [146]

Trump's threats are not just empty words but a danger to democracy and public safety. His modus operandi is clear: you are my enemy if you don't do as I say. Hitler operated this way, and Mafiosos did the same. This is the exact recipe for a wannabe autocrat who wants the law to align with his views rather than being based on the rule of law.

To give Trump *"a pass"* would probably be the worst possible course of action. He is undermining the law, eroding the international credibility of the U.S., and creating an almost free path for future coup attempts. However, deciding the appropriate punishment for Trump's numerous law violations is a complex challenge. It involves not only judicial but also political considerations. But time is also a crucial issue. In November 1923, Hitler attempted a coup but was imprisoned only a month later after a 25-day trial. Over three years after the January 6, 2021, insurrection, Trump still has yet to face trial.

CHAPTER 10

CONCERNS AND WARNINGS ABOUT TRUMP'S COMPETENCY AND MENTAL HEALTH FROM PEOPLE WHO KNOW HIM WELL

The best way to understand how Donald Trump functioned as president—and his capacity to hold another term—is to listen to the voices of those who know him well.

Mental health professionals have been warning for years about the danger of Trump's mental state, as described in the chapter about his personality. Additionally, an increasing number of voices have raised alarms about Trump's behavior and mental state from people who, through family relationships, work, or other associations, should have insightful perspectives on Trump as a person. The (not so?) shocking fact is that they all, in their own words, strongly warn against ever letting Donald Trump be president again.

Let's have a closer look at their concerns.

Starting with two family members;

Mary Trump, Donald Trump's niece, holds a master's degree and a Ph.D. in clinical psychology. She is also the daughter of Donald Trump's older brother. Here are some of her comments:

- *"Any way that a person can lie, cheat, and steal for his entire life, Donald Trump has."* (Hardball/MSNBC, May 6, 2019)
- *"Donald has no empathy, no interest in other persons—except to the extent that they can be of use to him."* (To MSNBC's Chris Hayes, September 18, 2021)
- *"Donald shows again that he cannot be trusted and doesn't care about this country or democracy. He is just happy he got away with it."* (About the insurrection on January 6, 2021, in an interview with MSNBC on April 7, 2022)
- *"People should know that Donald doesn't believe he should be denied anything he wants."* (MSNBC interview on June 16, 2022)
- She stated simply: *"He will kill democracy in the U.S. if he becomes elected president again in 2024."*

Author's note: Mary Trump has personal reasons for her negative feelings about her uncle, Donald Trump. She sued him, alleging that he defrauded her and her siblings of millions of dollars of family inheritance. This lawsuit is ongoing in the New York Supreme Court. Likewise, Donald Trump has filed a lawsuit against her for providing information about his taxes to the New York Times.

Their relationship is, to put it mildly, contentious. Please consider this context when evaluating her comments. However, her remarks align closely with those of others who know Donald Trump well.

Maryann Trump, another family member (Donald's older sister, an attorney, and a federal judge), has generally supported Donald. However, in late 2019, she revealed her true feelings through recorded conversations with her niece, Mary Trump. *"His goddamned tweet and the lying—Oh, my God,"* she expressed in one of the recordings. *"I'm talking too freely, but you know. The change of stories. The lack of preparation. The lying."*

At another point, she said: *"All he wants to do is appeal to his base. He has no principles. None."* She added: *"It's the phoniness and this cruelty. Donald is cruel."* *"You can't trust him,"* she said.[147]

Persons in various capacities and functions who have worked closely with Donald Trump over time.

The list is quite extensive, so I have arranged them in alphabetical order:

William ("Bill") Barr, Attorney General in the Trump administration, once likened Trump to a deranged character from Dr. Strangelove. *"He will always put his own interests ahead of everything else,"* Barr stated. When asked about Trump's fitness for the presidency if re-elected, Barr was candid: *"If you believe in his policies,* *what he is advertising as his policies, he's the last person who could actually execute them and achieve them. He lacks discipline, the capacity for strategic or linear thinking, setting priorities, or understanding how to get things done within the system; it's a horror show when he's left to his own devices. You may want his policies, but Trump won't deliver Trump policies. He will deliver chaos, and if anything, will lead to a backlash that will set his policies much further back than they otherwise would be."*

However, Barr made a surprising 180-degree turn in a May 2024 CNN interview, stating he would now support Donald Trump's presidential candidacy. So, Barr went from faithfully serving Trump in his first term to forcefully denouncing him to again supporting the man he claimed *"…will deliver chaos…"*. This might be what some would call a *"weathercock."* For lack of a better term, others have used *"coward."* However, behind Barr's latest reversal could lurk his fear of Trump's revenge for having opposed him in his last term.

John Bolton, former National Security Advisor in the Trump administration, said, *"The only thing DT cares about is DT. He doesn't know limits. It appalls me that DT could be elected president again. He doesn't comprehend the concepts of national interest and national security. His attention is short; he doesn't know much about world history. Xi Jinping, Putin, Kim Jong Un—I think they think he is a fool and are fully prepared to take advantage of him. He did damage in his first term; it has been largely repaired, but if he is elected to a second term, it might be irreparable."* In short, *"I think Trump is a danger to national security.*[148]

Does this seem like an arrogant statement from Bolton, who has worked with Trump on international security for under two years? I think not. What Bolton here points to is that Trump is grossly underestimating the minds of his *"friends"* like Putin.

To put this in perspective, look at what Illiarionov says about Putin in an interview with Kyiv Post in December 2023. (Illarionov was the chief economic adviser of Russian President Vladimir Putin for almost five years, from 2000 to December 2005.)[149]

The essence is that Putin is well-prepared, knowledgeable, a long-term strategist, and untrustworthy.

"Putin is very organized, well prepared, and spends much time not just finding out about the general picture but the details. Usually, he is so well prepared, at least in my time, as to what he will do that he has several options, versions, and scenarios. So, anybody that thinks he's out of touch—they are just purely incorrect. He is one of the best-prepared people for anything he will undertake. He started to prepare for the war against Georgia in Sept 1999 when he was Prime Minister, and he realized the scenario nine years later. He started to prepare for the war against Ukraine in 2003. And we have the full-fledged war in 2022, 19 years later. So that is a person not of a short-term solution but of a long-term strategy."

Q: *"If there are peace negotiations with Ukraine, do you think he can be trusted?"*

Illarionov: *"We know that he violated all agreements that either he himself or Russia signed with Ukraine. All documents: the bilateral treaty between Russia and Ukraine, the so-called big or grand treaty, the agreement on the creation*

> *of the CIS (Commonwealth of Independent States), the United Nations Charter, the Helsinki Act of 1975 to preserve stability, peace, and international borders in Europe, the Budapest Memorandum of 1994, the special agreement on the border between Russia and Ukraine, and so on. We don't have any document he would not violate. This should give an idea to anyone whether to trust, not only the oral word but also the written documents signed by Mr. Putin."*

Q: *"Why does the West misunderstand him?"*

Illarionov: *"I would not say all of them, but especially those making decisions and pursuing policy. They have a wrong understanding of the culture of that person. They are not accustomed to a situation where rules are violated all the time. Western leaders, to a certain extent, are accustomed to the rule of law and keeping promises, at least by leaders of other countries. They are not used to situations where any of these rules can be violated at any time. That is why they cannot fully understand their so-called 'partner' or adversary."*

Q: *"What is the most important lesson to learn about Putin?"*

Illarionov: *"He will move until he is stopped."*

Michael Cohen, Trump's former lawyer:

(Author's note: After working as Trump's closest lawyer for a decade, Michael Cohen was "thrown under the bus" by Trump for truthfully testifying about the Trump organization to Congress. It is well-known that Cohen now seeks revenge, and his revenge is the truth. Even if we discount some of his expressions, his revelations about Trump's personality and work ethic are alarming.)

To MSNBC in an interview on September 26, 2021:

"Even if Donald Trump is widely recognized as one of the biggest and most notorious liars of all time, on top of being narcissistic, millions of Americans believe him and follow him! But it would never have happened if social media and unscrupulous Republican leaders had not helped him." Michael Cohen points out a crucial fact here: *"…it would never have happened if not helped by social media and unscrupulous Republican leaders."* I comment more on this in other sections.

In an interview on the Midas Touch podcast on December 30, 2021, Cohen said:

"Everything that goes on in this [Trump] organization, you have to understand, it is corrupt, it is dirty, it is like a pig stall, and you have to go a bit deeper with all of them—Meadows included, Giuliani included, Josh Hawley included."

And: *"Donald Trump uses mob code. Not directly giving orders but hinting in a special way that is understood by his subordinates."*

To The New York Times on November 22, 2023, Cohen warned:

"Donald Trump is going to weaponize the DOJ and go after his critics: Milley, Barr, and lots of others."

Ty Cobb, lawyer, member of Trump's legal team July 2017 to May 2018:

"Delay is his major strategic objective in all these cases. Trump's constitutional objections to the trial-related issues are all frivolous," said a former Trump attorney, comparing the former president to a *"mob boss"* in a CNN interview in September 2023.

Jenna Ellis, **Trump's former lawyer,** pleaded guilty in the Georgia election subversion case. In October 2023, she stated: *"I simply can't support him for elected office again. Why I have chosen to distance myself is because of that frankly malignant narcissistic tendency to simply say that he's never done anything wrong."*

Mark Esper, former Defense Secretary in the Trump administration, stated in June 2023, *"I believe he [Trump] is not fit for office."*

James Comey, former FBI Director under Trump, said, *"Amoral leaders have a way of revealing the character of those around them. People lacking inner strength can't resist the compromises necessary to survive Mr. Trump, and that adds up to something they will never recover from. It takes a character like Mr. Mattis's to avoid the damage because Mr. Trump eats your soul in small bites"* (N.Y. Times, May 1, 2019).

Alyssa Farah Griffin, former White House director of strategic communications who resigned in early December 2020, weeks before the January 6 insurrection, called Trump *"a man unhinged, out of touch with reality"* in a CNN interview on June 29, 2022.

Stephanie Grisham, former White House Press Secretary, expressed her fears in an ABC News interview on October 4, 2021: *"I am terrified of him [Trump] running in 2024."*

Cassidy Hutchinson, former White House aide, said, *"I think that Donald Trump is the greatest threat that we will face to our democracy in our lifetime and potentially in American history."* In October 2023, she added, *"This year has helped me open my eyes to the dangers Trump actually poses to people in those situations."*

John Kelly, retired U.S. Marine Corps general and White House Chief of Staff, served in the Trump administration from July 2017 to December 2018. He stated, *"Donald Trump is the most flawed person I have ever met. He is a person who has no idea what America stands for and what America is all about. A person who admires autocrats and murderous dictators. He is not truthful regarding his position on the protection of unborn life, on women, on minorities, on Evangelical Christians, on Jews, on working men and women. Trump rants that our most precious heroes who gave their lives in America's defense are 'losers.' He would like to have military parades but without any wounded veterans. He has nothing but contempt for our democratic institutions, our Constitution, and the rule of law. God help us."*

Sarah Matthews, deputy press secretary for the Trump administration from June 2020 to January 2021, resigned the day after the January 6 insurrection. In an MSNBC interview on February 25, 2024, she said, *"If you had told me back when I resigned on Jan 6, 2021, that just a few short years later, Donald Trump would still be the leader of the Republican Party and be marching toward the GOP nomination for 2024, and that he would not be showing any remorse for Jan 6, I would be shocked."* She added, *"It seems crazy that* *he has doubled down on his election lie despite zero evidence of fraud."*

James Mattis, retired Marine General and Secretary of Defense in Trump's Cabinet said, *"Trump is the first president in my lifetime who does not try to unite the American people … Instead, he tries to divide us."* Mattis also stated, *"The former President Trump was more dangerous than you could ever imagine."*

H.R. McMaster, former National Security Adviser, fired by a tweet, remarked that Trump *"showed the absence of leadership."*

General Mark Milley, former Chairman of the Joint Chiefs of Staff, was *"certain that Trump had gone into a serious mental decline in the aftermath of the election,"* noting that he was *"screaming at officials and constructing his alternate reality about endless election conspiracies,"* according to Woodward and Costa in their book *"Peril."*

Leon Panetta, former Defense Secretary, CIA director, and White House Chief of Staff, described Trump's modus operandi as creating *"chaos and havoc."*

Barbara Res, former Trump Organization Vice President, noted that Donald Trump is *"creating hateful characteristics of political opponents—thereby creating a climate where political violence becomes closer."*

Anthony Scaramucci, who served as Communications Director in the White House (for a record short term of 11 days!) before being fired for controversial statements, had previously worked closely with Trump during the 2016 presidential campaign. Trump personally hired him to serve in the White House. Scaramucci warned, *"A fire alarm must go off if Donald Trump gets another term in the White House. He wants to damage the institutions of the American system and, most importantly, the system of Separation of Powers. He wants to remove the FCC licenses (cut off the airtime) for those he disagrees with. He makes his decisions based on his pride and his ego. Such decisions might very well turn out to be bad."* Scaramucci also labeled Trump as *"the domestic terrorist of the 21ˢᵗ century."*

Tony Schwarz (TONY), author of the book "The Art of the Deal." [150] In a speech at Oxford University ten days before the election, Schwartz detailed his concerns about Trump, explaining his decision to distance himself from the persona he had helped shape and define. *"I spent hundreds of hours on the phone with him and numerous interviews,"* Schwartz recalled.

"He has a stunningly short attention span. Trump was always about Trump. He had almost no interest in his then-wife and his children. More than any human being I have ever met, Trump has the ability to convince himself that whatever he's saying at any moment is true, or sort of true, or at least ought to be true."

"I believe Donald Trump represents a dangerous threat to the future of our planet. Looking back, I can see three distinct traits,

besides his inability to focus, that strike me as alarming when I imagine him as President of the U.S.:

- *His utter disregard for the truth and his lack of conscience.*
- *He is guided entirely by what he perceives as his immediate self-interest.*
- *His inability to admit that he's wrong about anything."*

When asked by students at Oxford University how Trump might react if he were losing, Schwartz replied, *"I do not expect him to go quietly into the night. Donald Trump is forever seeking attention the same way drug addicts seek another 'high.' He will resort to anger and rally his supporters by any means necessary to claim the election was rigged and that he didn't really lose. If Trump loses the election, he will not concede and will never acknowledge that he lost. This will lead to a dangerous, tense time in America."*

Schwartz concluded, *"Ultimately, I created Trump as far more winning than he is. I did not find him especially intelligent or exciting, but he was undeniably an effective self-promoter. I never saw any evidence that Trump had deep convictions or guiding core values, which helped explain why he could shift positions so effortlessly and unashamedly from one day to the next. Every belief of Trump struck me as negotiable for the right price or advantage. His most abiding passion was to prove that he was a winner.*

Friendships for Trump were purely functional. He was friendly to people who made his deals happen and unfriendly to those who stood in his way. Friendships came and went, just like his wives and girlfriends. His ideology: Whatever, as long as I win and people notice.

He grew up with a brutal father and a mother with whom he seemed to have no relationship. The hunger for unconditional love and acceptance exists in all of us, and its absence is always a source of suffering. Trump wears his most primitive instincts—his greed and grandiosity, his lust and his envy—right there on his sleeves. This book that I wrote for him has haunted and dogged me for more than thirty years."

Cliff Sims, former Special Assistant to Donald Trump and Director of White House Message Strategy, claims that Trump has created an "enemies list" comprising members of his administration.

Olivia Troye, former Homeland Security & Counterterrorism Adviser to VP Pence, described Trump as *"a deranged individual; he has no connection to reality"* in an MSNBC interview on January 19, 2022.

These voices, from people who know Trump well from working with him in key positions in his presidential period, paint a troubling picture of his character and the risks he poses if he were to hold office again.

Many others who have come close to Donald Trump in various capacities also raise grave concerns about a possible future Trump presidency:

Carl Bernstein, a Watergate reporter, political analyst, and author, said in a CNN interview on July 25, 2021: *"Trump is our own American war criminal."*

Maggie Haberman, political analyst and author of Trump's biography, describes Trump as a *"shallow,* *insecure, celebrity status seeker in a country that is increasingly celebrity-driven."* She refutes his image as a successful businessman, which she claims he was not, and calls him *"a walking national security risk."* Haberman highlights, *"It is very problematic when objective facts are no longer agreed upon in this country. That became clear in 2016, and it has evolved much since then. The clearest example is his election lie, which he repeats relentlessly."*

Steven Hassan, author of *"The Cult of Trump,"* comments on Trump's resilience even as criminal acts are revealed: *"It's a standard operating procedure for malignant narcissists. They are pathological liars, and they think they are above the law. His 40 million American base are the spiritual warriors that Mike Flynn is tapping into."*

David Cay Johnston, Pulitzer Prize–winning author, says: *"There are, in broad terms, mainly two kinds of people that are emerging in this Trump era: Those who show principles and resolve and those who choose expediency over principles."*

David Jolly, attorney and former Republican, said on June 1, 2023: *"Donald Trump is a brutish, transactional politician who will walk into a room, try to crush the Constitution, likely fail, and be stopped by the courts."*

Mark Leibovich, the author, is similarly brutal in his assessments: *"Trump has a way of wearing you down,"* he observes. *"He invades your habitat, like the opossum that gets into the attic, dies, stinks, and attracts derivative nuisances."*

Glenn Kirschner, lawyer and former federal prosecutor, remarked: *"Donald Trump has never been in the presidency for the good of the people, the nation's safety, or the well-being of our military. He is in it for himself, what he can get out of it."*

Julia Ioffe, a Russian-born and raised Russian-American journalist and author, said in an interview with Frontline PBS in January 2023: *"After the 2016 presidential election, which Trump won with undeniable and proven help from Russia, Putin was delighted. 'His' man had won. According to one of President Medvedev's higher-ranked advisors, Trump was, in 2020, seen as 'a wrecking ball—our wrecking ball.' "A man who had disrupted America's faith in themselves. The Russian leadership was pleased to see how Trump undermined NATO and how he led the U.S. into internal conflicts, culminating with the attack on Congress on Jan 6, 2021. Thus leaving the European scene easier for Russia to control."*[151]

Michael Lustig, a former federal judge, said on November 4, 2023: *"Now, 2 1/2 years after the Jan 6 insurrection, former President Trump is a clear, present, and imminent danger to American democracy."*

Rick Wilson, a Republican strategist and author of Everything Trump Touches Dies," warned: *"If Trump is elected again, there will be chaos, authoritarianism, violence, and the end of the U.S. constitutional republic. Trump will certainly be the Republican nominee. Sixty percent of his base worships him as if he were a god. They don't accept criticism; they are not looking for ideological change because Trump is post-ideological.*

He is a spectacle, a transgressor, and they want that. It makes him unbeatable inside his base. But the picture is different outside, and Donald will be blown out. If Trump becomes the Republican nominee, you can expect the most hideous, negative campaign in the history of world politics. Trump has to be elected to the presidency to stay out of jail. Trump has nothing to lose. No boundaries, no guardrails, no nothing."

Bob Woodward, a Watergate reporter, political analyst, and author, shared his insights after eight hours of direct interviews with Trump, seven years studying Trump's presidency, and writing three books about him. On August 3, 2023, he said, *"He doesn't understand the presidency and the responsibilities that come with it. He just doesn't get it. Everything is about him. He simply believes, 'Everything is mine.'"* He also drew a parallel between Nixon's Watergate and Trump's efforts to overturn a presidential election, emphasizing a lust for political power. *"But in the case of Trump, it is not just political power, but personal power,"* Woodward noted.

In a CNN interview on October 23, 2022, Woodward stated, *"He is not only not the right man for the job; he is dangerous, and he's a threat to democracy, and he is a threat to the presidency because he doesn't understand the core obligations that come with that office."* Further, in another CNN interview in June 2023, Woodward remarked, *"I think Donald Trump regards democracy as enemy territory because it is about other people. And he likes everything to be about him."*

Despite all warnings, Trump commands a major political party and enjoys broad support from the American public. This situation has been compared to that of former U.K. Prime Minister Boris Johnson. Norway's second-largest newspaper, Dagbladet, made this comparison: *"Two right-wing opportunists following their own rules. They encouraged discord and chaos. Both were infamous for being narcissistic ego-trippers and women abusers long before they entered the political stage. They are both known as liars and cheaters."*[152]

"However, the comparison has its limits. Boris Johnson was forced to resign as Prime Minister in July 2022 and as a parliament member a year later due to deep mistrust of his actions and behavior. On both occasions, he claimed it was a result of a "witch-hunt."

Will the broader public come to understand and accept the dangerous consequences of Donald Trump's narcissistic behavior? Or will his constant lies and propaganda continue to deafen and blind them? And what about the intimidated Republican leadership? Will they persist in standing on the wrong side of decency?

CHAPTER 11

TRYING TO UNDERSTAND TRUMP'S POPULARITY

Why has Trump managed to secure such an extensive base of voters and a timid flock of Republican leaders that support him no matter what?

I must admit that initially, I was drawn to Trump's unconventional approach to political problems. One notable example is his engagement with Kim Jong Un in North Korea. Any attempt at dialogue with such a dictator seemed futile, but Trump took a leap, initiated contact, and started a (short-lived) dialogue. Perhaps, in his unconventional way, Trump could bridge two different worlds. My background as a business leader also influenced my belief in him as a business leader. However, the dialogue quickly became farcical, revealing Trump's naiveté.

Another aspect that initially intrigued me was Trump's claim of being a *"self-made"* billionaire. However, it soon became apparent that Trump's wealth was initially created by his father, who provided capital and loans to launch Trump into the real estate business. Additionally, upon closer inspection of his business practices, it became evident that bankruptcies and shady dealings were part of his modus operandi.

Thus, my participation in Trump's popularity club was relatively short-lived.

However, Trump's popularity among millions did not arise from nowhere. Deep discontentment—exacerbated by tremendous income and wealth inequalities in American society, creates a widespread feeling that *"the system is against us."* In such an environment, Trump's repeated claims to *"drain the swamp"* (which he never did during his presidential term) had massive appeal, especially for white disenfranchised people. They, along with many others, are desperate for a savior. The needs and reasons vary, from tax cuts for the wealthy to promises of a better life for those feeling betrayed by the government. Trump's oratory skills and promises perfectly matched their hopes and frustrations.

The need for change and its reasons are genuine and should be taken seriously. Hillary Clinton made a huge mistake by showing no respect for Trump's followers when she referred to them as *"deplorable."* JP Morgan CEO Jamie Dimon wisely pointed out that scapegoating MAGA Trump supporters because they like him is wrong, both morally and factually.

They vote for Trump because they support his policies (on immigration, abortion, etc.), not necessarily because they endorse his values. Dimon says, *"He may be morally bankrupt, but I like his policy."*

The question becomes: How low a social morale and social conscience should we accept from a national leader if we align with their policies? Ignore it? That seems to be an accepted and common idea in Republican circles.)

Trump's tax policies have secured the support of the wealthy elite, who largely seem to endorse him no matter his character or ambitions, as long as he serves their purpose. His immigration stance has caught a large part of the white population who feel their rights are seriously threatened and are willing to skip the moral side as long as they can get help. And the fact that Trump is the leader of the Republican Party is in itself a crucial factor for collecting nationwide votes, regardless of his personality.

But Trump's widespread popularity also stems from a variety of reasons not closely tied to his political policies.

Ten apparent reasons that have helped Donald Trump become and remain popular despite his rude behavior and fairly independent of his policies:

1. *"The Apprentice"*: The show made Trump a national figure and TV personality with star status, attracting interest and admiration.
2. His Image: As a *"self-made"* millionaire and successful businessman.
3. Wealth Perception: He is seen as someone who, being well-off, knows how to handle the wealthy

elite. This might be why many not-so-wealthy people believe he can be their spokesperson.

4. Angering the *"Right"* People: For those who feel the system has screwed them, Trump insults the elites who are perceived as doing great while wages are stagnant, and they talk down to the ordinary people.

5. The Big Lie: His ability to lie and his strategy of repeating lies to persuade people.

6. Entertainment factor: In 2016, Jeb Bush was cautious and almost dull, while Obama was always well-articulated and polite. On the other hand, Trump was unpredictable and straightforward, which many found entertaining.

7. Nostalgia: People want 2019 back, not necessarily Trump, but a time without COVID and the Russia-Ukraine war.

8. Charisma: His anti-political establishment language, calling Washington leaders *"the swamp,"* resonated with many middle and lower-class people who felt neglected by the well-off politicians.

9. False Impressions: Many believe he sides with average Joe and Jane in economic matters. Unfortunately, his policies have favored the more well-off, particularly in areas like taxes and social security.

10. Christians, particularly evangelical Christians, surprisingly have a firm belief in Trump.[153] Odd, given his quite un-Christian display—but essential reasons are,

- They believe that he is not lying about the 2020 election.
- They like a *"strongman"* who they believe can stand against threats from an increasing non-white population.
- Many believe that he is sent from God.
- And they vote Republican.

Psychologist Joseph Burgo candidly explains why Trump's simplistic, rude, and "us-vs-them" has such a wide resonance among the public: *"In times of enormous demographic shift and economic uncertainty, populism exerts a strong appeal for the anxious voter. Populist messages rely on simplistic answers to complex problems and promote an us-versus-them warfare mentality. Like Mr. Trump, populists engaged in battle have traditionally ridiculed their opposition, but in the narcissistic endeavor to prove himself a winner at the expense of all those 'losers,' Trump relies on righteous indignation, blame, and contempt as weapons of war. Many disaffected voters are drawn to him precisely because of those traits and not in spite of them"*.

CHAPTER 12

TRUMP'S SUPPORTER BASE— THREE LAYERS

Layer 1: The Republicans in general.

Trump's main base is, of course, Republicans. Most Republicans have a strong or primarily favorable opinion of Trump. Interestingly, an in-depth analysis from 2021 indicates that the Republican Party can be split into four main groups: *"Faith & Flag Conservatives"* (the evangelicals), *"Populist Right"* (anti-establishment/anti-elite Republicans), *"Committed Conservatives,"* and *"Ambivalent Right."*[154] The analysis showed that the two first groups have two things in common: they strongly support Trump, and most believe Trump definitely or probably is the legitimate winner of the 2020 election. According to the study, these two groups comprise more than half of Republican voters, while the others comprise about 30%. This means Trump has a very firm stronghold among Republican voters. (The study did not account for the remaining

15-20%.) However, the share of Republicans who view Trump favorably has decreased by almost 10 % from 2021/2022, when 75% viewed him favorably.[155]

Layer 2: The MAGA movement and its supporters.

Trump was not the first to use the MAGA slogan. The Republican President Ronald Reagan used *"Let's Make America Great Again"* as one of several slogans for his 1980 presidential campaign. In 2012, Trump managed to register *"Make America Great Again as a trademark to "promote public awareness of political issues and fundraising in the field of politics."* [156] He announced the slogan on the same day that he declared his candidacy for the 2016 Republican presidential nomination on June 16, 2015—the beginning of the MAGA movement.

MAGA movement origins, meaning, and beliefs.

"Make America Great Again," or *"MAGA,"* became a rallying cry for Trump supporters. It is founded on the belief that the United States was once a *"great"* country but has lost this status because of foreign influence, pointing to immigration, multiculturalism, and *"bad international trade deals."* MAGA supporters believe this decline can be reversed through "America first" policies like economic protectionism, reducing or halting immigration, particularly from developing countries, and enforcing what they consider to be traditional American values. In 2018, Reuters asked 1,249 Trump supporters what MAGA

meant to them. Here is what they answered, in ranking order:[157]

- Better economy
- Stronger borders
- Lower taxes
- Better international agreements
- Donald Trump (!)
- Conservative judges
- More freedom
- Anti-immigrant

Initially, Trump's unorthodox and brash style falsely portrayed him as a man of the people. His emphasis on themes like immigration and anti-establishment, coupled with his abrasive demeanor, began to gain traction. Consequently, his MAGA supporter base expanded to include *"ordinary"* individuals grappling with economic challenges, lured by Trump's grandiose promises of a better economy. The support of right and far-right believers also played a crucial role in securing Trump's victory in the 2016 election.

During his presidency, Trump took several actions to please his MAGA base. For instance, he issued executive orders attempting to ban immigration from seven Muslim-majority countries (which were later rejected by the courts as discriminatory, though he made subsequent attempts). Additionally, he signed an order to initiate *"the immediate construction of a physical wall on the southern border with Mexico."* He also imposed tariffs on imports from several countries, including China, the European Union,

Mexico, and Canada. Consequently, the MAGA base appeared relatively content with his actions.

But what about tax reductions? Oh, sorry, those were implemented for the wealthy and big corporations, purportedly to stimulate economic growth that would trickle down to you, the MAGA base. (However, direct wealth redistribution from the affluent to the less privileged is rare. Some economic benefits may indirectly reach lower-income individuals through job creation.) Lastly, three ultra-conservative Supreme Court justices were appointed during his term, solidifying a conservative majority on the bench. Overall, these actions appeared sufficient to maintain his broader base's support.

In 2020, Trump lost the election but convinced his supporter base that it was stolen from him. This deepened the political divide among Americans,

Losing the 2020 election hurt his self-image of a *"never-loser"* so much that he never admitted his loss and claimed the election was *"stolen."* And as this was not enough, he was instrumental in planning and executing the Jan 6 insurrection, supported mainly by his accomplices and a strong supporter base.[158]

This created a new and dangerous situation in the political landscape. The customary differences in political opinions and perspectives, marked by lively, sometimes contentious debates, were now polarized into stark contrasts. President Bush's words from 2001, *"Either you are with us, or you are with the terrorists,"* took on a new dimension: *"You are either with Trump or not. If not, we are willing to fight."* The perceived adversary suddenly became domestic rather than foreign—a reality acknowledged by both sides. A dangerous trend began to emerge. Political divisions among Americans became uncompromising and unforgiving, fueled by Trump's active role in the Capitol attack, characterized by inflammatory rhetoric. This fostered a hostile climate and heightened tensions.

Right-wing and far-right-wing ideologies gained traction, with Trump's hardline stance as a catalyst. Racist, homophobic, and sexist content proliferated on social media, with an alarming increase in posts inciting violence.

Who inspired them?—Did I hear Donald Trump?

A political division had been brewing but is now boiling over.

What separates MAGA supporters from other Republicans?

Based on six different polls conducted between 2020 and 2024, a clear pattern of the differences between MAGA Republicans and non-MAGA Republicans emerges:[159]

- Donald Trump is the President! Almost 90% of MAGA Republicans believe Biden is not the legitimately elected president, while acceptance of Biden is much higher among non-MAGA Republicans.
- More evangelical and conservative: MAGA Republicans tend to be more evangelical and more conservative.
- Weaker allegiance to the Republican Party: Their loyalty is less intense. If Trump had his polit-

ical party, they would support it more than the Republican Party.

- Unlikely to vote Democratic: Under no circumstances are they likely to vote for the Democratic Party. The 2022 House election showed that up to 10% of non-MAGA Republicans "crossed over," while only 2% of MAGA supporters did.
- Devotion to Trump: A clear majority of MAGA Republicans say they aren't at all concerned about Trump's indictments, compared to 39% of non-MAGA supporters.
- Belief in extreme views: Higher belief in views considered extreme, like anti-vaccine sentiments and conspiracy theories.

MAGA supporters seem unified about at least three beliefs:

- The 2020 election was *"stolen"* from Trump through massive voter fraud.
- *"Forces are changing our country for the worse."*
- *"The American way of life is threatened."*

Other beliefs widely held within the MAGA circles:[160]

- More restrictions on voting: To avoid what they perceive as massive fraud.
- Mainstream news is *"fake news."*
- Various conspiracy theories:

- The Jan 6 riot was the work of ANTIFA, not Trump supporters.
- COVID-19 is a bioweapon from China.
- Immigration is changing American culture for the worse.
- Immigration policies aim to replace Americans with non-white immigrants (*"replacement theory"*).
- Extreme beliefs: Some hardcore MAGA supporters even believe Biden is dead, Trump is the natural leader of the military, and other outlandish theories. These beliefs range from wild to wilder and, ultimately, dangerous.
- *"QAnon"*: The belief that former President Trump is waging a secret war against Satan-worshipping pedophiles in government, business, and the media.

At the far right of the MAGA base, there are militant groups like the Proud Boys, the Oath Keepers, and the Three Percenters, willing to use weapons to seize power. This brings to mind the authoritarian warning from **Matthew MacWilliams**, who studied the MAGA movement in 2015. He noted, *"In fact, I've found a single statistically significant variable that predicts whether a voter supports Trump—and it's not race, income, or education levels: It's authoritarianism."* He continued, *"Authoritarians obey. They rally to and follow strong leaders.* And they respond aggressively to outsiders, especially when they feel threatened. From pledging to *"make America great again" by building a wall on the border to promising to close mosques and ban Muslims from visiting the United States, Trump is playing directly to author-*

itarian inclinations." He concluded in 2015 that *"it's very possible that Trump's fan base will continue to grow."* [161]

MAGA supporters—who are they?

Their political views are mainly right or far-right wing. Research shows, perhaps surprising for many, that MAGA supporters are not typically lower middle-class workers but a less homogenous group than many realize. Roughly half earn at least $50,000 annually, so they're considered middle-income by many standards, and approximately one-third have at least a college degree. The results from *"The Panel Study of MAGA Supporters in 2020/2021"* [162]indicated that the demographic composition of the MAGA movement is overwhelmingly white, male, Christian, retired, and over 65 years of age.

Groups advocating for gun rights are prevalent among MAGA supporters. Other prominent affiliations include charities, pro-police groups, anti-lockdown movements, pro-life advocates, and *"stop the steal"* organizations. These groups are predominantly aligned with the Republican Party.

I came across an opinion from L. Cohen on Quora. His comment may contain elements of truth but also shows a distant and somewhat hollow understanding of MAGA supporters, who primarily consist of people who have felt overlooked and excluded. Many have struggled to get by in life and have faced the challenges of poverty, even as the current president regularly claims things are improving, which often isn't the case for the average American. While Cohen's comment is partly factual, it is undeniably mocking and slightly humorous. I include it here for the latter reason, hoping MAGA supporters can see the humor and seriousness of the matter.

He said:

"I think they (MAGA) fall into three groups:

- *People wealthy enough to benefit from his tax and regulatory cuts (health, safety, environmental, consumer fairness, etc.) for their companies. This is a small number of people.*
- *Racists and xenophobes who love how Trump throws out ethnic and racial slurs (Mexican immigrants are rapists, keep all Muslims out, fine people among the neo-Nazis, etc.).*
- *Dimwits who fall for his macho rhetoric, facts be damned. They, like Trump, have no idea what treason is or who pays tariffs (they do). They love the way Trump denigrates people with actual expertise in government or science. They have no idea how valuable natural allies are and how vile the autocrats that Trump loves are. The evangelicals are in this category."*

Many struggle with immigration because they've lost their jobs to foreigners, been victims of crimes committed by foreigners, or know someone who has. All in all, MAGA supporters cover a broad spectrum of people, many in the middle-income bracket, who feel American politicians have been on the *"wrong track."* They see Donald Trump as a *"strongman"* outside the establishment, capable of fixing everything.

Did he meet their expectations during his presidency? As seen above, he did not live up to many of his promises.

However, he started building the border wall, increased levies on imports from China and other countries, and helped ensure conservative dominance in the Supreme Court. But did *"the man in the street"* see improvements in their economic situation during his term? Unfortunately, not.

MAGA supporters. How many?

MacWilliams seems to have been correct about the numbers and the authoritarian tendencies of their leader, Donald Trump. The MAGA movement grew steadily from 2016 until 2022, becoming a significant political force in America. In late 2022, 40% of Republicans identified as *"MAGA Republicans."* However, the numbers have since stagnated, even diminished from there, parallel to Trump's ever-increasing hardliner rhetoric and his problems with the law. And the popularity seems to dwindle, although not much. As of April 2023, only 24% of Americans had favorable views of the MAGA movement, 45% negative. [163]

Is this a possible sign that Americans are growing tired of the hate and revenge rhetoric delivered by Trump?

Within the broad spectrum of people believing in Trump, there are smaller groups whose belief in Trump has reached a cult level:

Layer 3: The MAGA cult.

Within the MAGA movement, there is a core cult of *"die-hard"* believers who follow anything their leader suggests or commands. These believers are visible at Trump rallies and on social media but are estimated to comprise only a tiny part of the movement. Some estimates suggest 1%, but could be higher.

"Cult"—isn't that a term used only for religious sects and fanatics? The answer is no; it is also used more generally. A standard definition is:

*"…**People who practice excessive devotion to a figure, object, or belief system, typically following a charismatic leader.**"* [164]

These groups do much of the *"dirty work"* to scare anyone or anything that gets in their leader's way. When talking about the Trump cult, there are numerous examples of how they follow Trump's increasing aggressiveness by threatening and intimidating people perceived as his *"enemies."* A particularly alarming example comes from the E. Carroll sex abuse and defamation case: After the jury verdict, the judge advised the nine jurors to *"never disclose that you were on this jury."* This is a unique statement in a U.S. court but reflects the numerous incidents of Trump threatening prosecutors, judges, court staff, and witnesses. It has become apparent that if you are against Trump in a court case, you risk being a victim of his rage via his most ardent followers.

Quotes from *"die-hard"* MAGA fans:

Let me illustrate their fanaticism with some examples, which, in many cases, might seem *"wild"* or *"ridiculous."* Nonetheless, some of these statements can lead to dangerous actions driven by a passionate belief.

- From TikTok account *"Hey MAGA 2024"*: When a young MAGA fan was asked, *"What would you rather have—four more years of Donald Trump as a dic-*

tator or four more years of Joe Biden as president?" he responded, *"I think I am choosing Donald Trump as a dictator for four more years."*

- *"All you have heard [about Trump] is lies."* (Comment from a Trump supporter on an MSNBC YouTube clip.) Comments on Facebook from devoted DT fans—

September 2023:

- *"AMEN, PRESIDENT TRUMP LETS TAKE BACK OUR COUNTRY AND MAKE IT THE BEST ITS EVER BEEN WITH YOUR HELP!!!!!!!!!!!!!!"*
- *"Way to go, MR PRESIDENT. GOD BLESS YOU, OUR NEXT PRESIDENT, 2024. MAKE AMERICA GREAT AGAIN."*
- *"Thanks for who you are and being willing to support us and doing what's right!!!! Love you, President Trump!! ★!"*
- *"Yes Absolutely Praise God Hallelujah*

Direct transcription from video interviews:

A young woman: *"I am willing to die for Trump."*

A middle-aged woman wearing a T-shirt that says, *"I am a Trump girl,"* was asked in March 2024, *"Who is president?"* She answered, *"Trump is President. There are a lot of things this Mr. Biden doesn't have, like the presidential seal and things like that. It's pretty obvious."* When the reporter pointed out, *"When President Biden speaks, there is a pres-*

idential seal right in front of him," she quickly responded, *"Not real."*

Another exchange occurred with an older adult wearing a Trump cap and a T-shirt covered with Trump images:

- Reporter: *"What is he (Trump) doing as president?"*
- Man: *"He is in charge of the military. The military is in charge of the whole thing."*
- A woman chimed in: *"The military put him in charge in 2018 when President Trump signed an executive order."*
- Reporter: *"The military arms going to Ukraine, we have Donald Trump to thank for that?"*
- (Short pause): *"Nooo."*
- Reporter: *"So, there are two militaries, the good and the bad one?"*
- Man: *"Yes. There's the good and the bad."*
- Reporter: "So, Trump is in charge of the good one?" Man: *"Yes."*
- Reporter: *"Biden is in charge of the bad military?"*
- Man: *"Yes, that is exactly right."*
- A female Trump fan told an interviewer, *"He (Trump) never lied to the American people. He always told us the truth."* Another woman added, *"I know it in my heart. I know it in my spirit. He (Trump) has never lied about anything."*

Comments like these remind me of Mark Twain's observation: *"It is easier to fool people than to convince them they have been fooled."*

Or, as Dr. Bandy Lee states: *"When the mind is hijacked for the benefit of the abuser, it becomes no longer a matter of presenting facts or appealing to logic."*[165]

Dr. Steven Hassan can explain how cults form, drawing from his experience. As a college student, he was brainwashed to become a Moon cult member and says he would have killed his parents if asked. After escaping, he now recognizes how Trump has used similar brainwashing methods to create a MAGA cult within the more significant MAGA movement:

1. Create confusion by overloading with information faster than people can digest. Cult leaders establish themselves as heroes who have the solutions to complex problems, providing meaning and hope outside of existing institutional structures. They speak to people's emotions rather than critical thinking, creating a sense of certainty.

2. Convince people quickly. Previously, this could have been a long process involving face-to-face interactions, individually and in groups. It happens faster than ever, thanks to social media and algorithms that favor controversial posts, speeding up, accentuating, and cementing extreme opinions.

3. Follow a systematic process. The transformation into a cult follower can be described by a model that applies to various movements, whether it's MAGA, sex traffickers, or Hitler's *"Der Fuhrer"* cult. There are specific actions and certain "buttons" to push.

Dr. Hassan compares Donald Trump to Jim Jones, the Moon sect leader. According to Hassan, Trump and his team, have identified key groups of people and each group's unique vulnerabilities. They gathered a lot of data about American citizens. Religious groups, anti-abortion groups, people in favor of keeping the gun laws, patriot groups, etc. For each group, they designed which *"buttons"* messages to convey to transform members of these groups through a systematic social influence process. Dr. Hassan says there are certain *"control buttons."* [166]

With the help of social media, this transformation can be very rapid. For instance, Alex Jones might start a story propagated by Breitbart Media and be picked up by Fox News, spreading it widely across social media. Thus, Trump's cult status is not merely a result of his natural charisma as a demagogue but also a well-prepared and well-designed marketing plan targeting the most susceptible groups of Americans.

Dr. Hassan warns that narcissistic cult leaders threatened by the law can be very dangerous. He uses Jim Jones as an example, who, when exposed, ordered the killing of his cult members and Congressman Leo Ryan. It is alarming to see Donald Trump now in a similar situation, escalating from mocking to more threatening rhetoric. While Dr. Hassan remains optimistic, he stresses that we must *"open our eyes and roll up our sleeves."*

Statements by Republican leaders are not only encouraging but also inflaming the MAGA cult members:

Observing that even most elected Republican Congress members are signaling acceptance of Trump's and his core MAGA base's dangerous actions and rhetoric, I do not share Dr. Hassan's optimism. However, one can hope for a change. Republican leaders have flipped the value system from prioritizing Country and Constitution above Party and Power to placing Party and Power above Country and Constitution. Intelligent but power-hungry delegates like Ted Cruz and Josh Hawley and outspoken figures like Marjorie Taylor Greene and Matt Gaetz lead this shift. Unless these and many other Republican Congress members *"flip back"* and signal this to their constituents, the political future of the country and the Republican Party seems bleak. Cults and authoritarians cannot become a force without leaders and collaborators.

Can cult members be persuaded to *"quit"*? Not easily. If you have family or friends who have become cult members, Dr. Hassan advises educating yourself on the subject if you want to help. He has developed an *"Influence Continuum Model"* that shows how people are persuaded into hard-core beliefs.

Dr. Hassan emphasizes building rapport and trust to reach out to individuals displaying cult-like attitudes. Do not block them out or call them derogatory names. The last thing to do is call them morons, deplorables, immoral, idiots, etc. Instead, ask questions and listen to their answers. Build bridges, control your reactivity, and ask for facts.

Examples of disillusioned hard-core MAGA fans:

Steve Deace (podcaster, *"Steve Deace Show"*):

"When you like being called a schmuck and ask for more, that's when it is a cult. I was a sucker. I wanted to be such. And I resented the person who tried to get me out of that. How many of you sent money to the 'Stop the Steal' campaign three years ago? How many shows have I wasted your time talking about this three years ago? I still have not recovered from the election fraud lie and COVID-19 deception. I probably have the smallest FB crowd of any major show in this industry. Now Rudy Giuliani says, 'Yeah, I was lying.' And what does Jason Miller say now? 'We all know it was BS.'"

Pam Hemphill, a former *"Die Hard"* Trump fan who served two months in prison for participating in the January 6 insurrection:

"Biden is right when saying 'Donald Trump is a dangerous narcissist. He is a cult leader; he needs to be put in prison. He is not any different than Epstein, his friend who killed himself in prison. Trump is disgusting. When you threaten the judge or the Secretary of State and want to do a swat on somebody, it's terrifying. And the narrative is getting worse and worse. And I hold Trump totally responsible."

The Authoritarian leader: Persuasive but in need of followers to reinforce his delusions.

An authoritarian leader needs his devoted followers, enablers, and collaborators; without them, he is nothing. Similarly, every cult needs an authoritarian leader. A cult is a perfect symbiosis between an autocratic leader and his followers.

Authoritarian leaders like Trump have the ability, talent, and drive to communicate ten times more than anyone else. Ten times more often, ten times more words than his opponents. This type of leader constantly messages. You don't see Biden doing that. Trump, however, is the modern-times *"star example"* of utilizing social media to the extreme. Psychologist Bill Eddy describes it like this:

"Constantly talking in emotional terms, using what I call The Fantasy Crisis Triad:

1. There is a terrible crisis.
2. An evil villain (group or person) is causing this crisis.
3. I am the hero, going to save you from this terrible crisis and this evil person or persons." *"…* *Trump "classic: "Only I can fix it." "…This type of leader doesn't have the knowledge, skills, and knowledge required for government and politics. So they always come in as outsiders, claiming to be heroes. And to be that, they need to have a crisis, a fantasy, or something they created by themselves that could be real, and then get into power with that."* [167]

When I hear this description by Mr. Eddy, my thoughts immediately turn to Hitler a hundred years ago and Trump now. You could call this *"How to Rise to Power."* But this is a *"road trip"* only possible for persons with an extreme drive for power, an extreme belief in their greatness, an extreme energy level—and charisma, the intuitive ability to reach the masses emotionally. We also find these traits in other authoritarians/dictators like Chavez in Venezuela, Mao in China, and Stalin and Putin in Russia. To quote Eddy again: *"It is not about politics; it's about the personality."*

What people are susceptible to being in a cult or following a cult-like leader?

We all experience periods when we are more receptive to specific ideas. The death of a loved one, illness, losing a job, the pandemic, and economic problems are significant susceptibility factors. During these moments, we are more likely to listen to and accept ideas that bring hope. Trump's appeals about grandiosity, making America great again, restoring democracy, and *"draining the swamp"* are, for many, just what they need. These appeals are tempting but deceptive. Cult members go a giant step further. They stop thinking critically and adopt the leader's ideas as a kind of religion, almost holy, not to be questioned or criticized.

A cult member is characterized by an inability to see their leader's faults. In a cult, people have a black-and-white, good-versus-bad, all-or-nothing mindset. They are controlled through fear and manipulation of information. However, the real sign of a cult member is their inability to consider that their leader could be harmful or wrong. Only a tiny fraction of all MAGA supporters are in this cult mindset. Most of the 74 million Americans who voted for Trump in 2020 were Republicans who liked his tax policies, immigration, etc.

The violent extremes within the extremes.

An article in the Norwegian newspaper "VG" on March 25, 2024, featured an interview with Matt Browning and his wife Tony, who were undercover cops for 25 years among supremacist militia and violent extremist groups. Based on their experiences, they wrote the book *"The Hate Nextdoor."* This book shows how the combination of ideology and rhetoric has fueled violence among extreme groups in the U.S. for decades. Trump became a leader for these groups by aligning with the extreme right and inspiring more extremists. The border issue is a prime example. The rhetoric from people in power legitimizes violent actions. There are *"hunting teams"* traveling to the border to hunt down refugees. This could never happen on this scale without the *"authorization"* from leading politicians like Trump.

The Proud Boys would have killed Mike Pence and Nancy Pelosi if they had found them. Does anyone still think this is not a dangerous development?

CHAPTER 13

PROJECT 2025. HIS PLANS AND POLICIES, IF EVER AGAIN A SECOND TERM. AN IMMINENT DANGER FOR DEMOCRACY!

Former President Trump's second-term proposals signal a far-right conservative agenda with an unprecedented expansion of federal and presidential power. He aims to fire *"radical left"* officials, reshape the Justice Department to serve his interests and create an administration where disloyalty to the president is not tolerated. His explicit goal appears to be establishing authentic authoritarian leadership beyond the reach of the law.

Five ways from democracy to autocracy.

Nonsense? I don't think so. It's starting to resemble the situation Stuart Stevens describes in his book *"The Conspiracy to End America: Five Ways My Old Party is Driving*

Democracy to Autocracy," where he outlines five elements present when democracies transform into autocracies:

The support of a significant Party:

Trump's expressed authoritarian intentions have the support of the majority of the Republican Party. The Congress-elected Republicans are now a mix: some are too intimidated to oppose Trump, others are morally blinded by their love of power and will go along with anything Trump wants, and still others prioritize the Party above all else, no matter the cost.

A legal system to justify it:

There is a fight in the courts, with Trump's lawyers arguing for complete presidential immunity. Trump has the Supreme Court "on his side" with a conservative majority. A president wholly convinced he is above the law: If re-elected, he would have the power to instruct the Justice Department to drop any charges against him, including those pending in courts.

Propagandists, i.e., media carrying right-wing views:

National media, dominated by Fox News, and social media platforms like X, Meta, YouTube, TikTok, and others are powerful tools for spreading propaganda, making it increasingly difficult to distinguish between true and false information. A new and fast-growing problem is the severe threat of misinformation facilitated by AI algorithms.

Financiers:

There seem to be enough billionaires to support Donald Trump, including Peter Thiel, the Koch brothers, the Mercer family, and many others who back his ideas.

Shock Troops:

The Proud Boys, the Three Percenters, the Oath Keepers, and similar groups have shown their willingness to kill for Trump, as evidenced on January 6, 2021. Donald Trump, an almost fanatical, power-seeking demagogue, appears more than happy to exert total political power.

Let's hear what Donald Trump says himself:

On April 13, 2020: *"Somebody who is President of the United States has total authority. And that's the way it's going to be."*

On another occasion: *"Let me tell you something: If we don't get what we want, one way or the other, whether it's through you, through the military, anything you wanna call, I'll shut down the government."*

Or as he stated on his Truth Social platform: *"A PRESIDENT OF THE UNITED STATES MUST HAVE FULL IMMUNITY ...EVEN IN EVENTS THAT 'CROSS THE LINE.'"*

"Democracies have crumbled before, and that's on the verge of happening here," says Mary Guy, a professor at the University of Colorado Denver's School of Public Affairs.

"Project 2025." Far-right Republicans' and Trump's vision for a second term.

"Project 2025" was launched in April 2022 by the Heritage Foundation (a conservative think tank, a broad coalition of 50 conservative organizations heavily staffed by former Trump officials and loyalists), a plan for the next conservative president of the United States. Main goal: *"To defeat the anti-American left—at home and abroad,"* according to Kevin D. Roberts, the president of the Foundation. Their website paints a rather rosy picture of their plans.[168]

However, a closer look at the realities may present another color than a rose. Based on the abovementioned project, details have emerged from various sources that paint an accurate picture of what may lie ahead if Donald Trump gets a second presidential term.[169]

Viewed through democratic lenses, the picture is not pleasant. The balance of powers will be disrupted. Currently, presidents usually rely on Congress to implement policies. Project 2025 implies that Congress cannot limit the president's control over the executive branch. Professor Peter Strauss of Columbia University Law School says this approach is a fundamentally misguided— and limited—interpretation of the Constitution. *"The Constitution can only properly be understood as making the president the overseer of the government that Congress creates, not its commander,"* he says. *"The president is the military commander, but the power explicitly defined for him over ordinary domestic government is much less."*

Key points of "Project 2025."

Workforce.

The goal is to create a workforce loyal to the president rather than the Constitution. How? Place loyalists in significant legal and executive positions—Jeff Sessions and Billy Barr are probably not malleable enough! This includes the appointment of attorneys and personnel who would be willing to push through controversial aspects of Trump's agenda. The authority to hire and fire federal workers at will is part of this strategy. These plans include reshaping the Department of Justice, firing thousands of civil workers, [170]and ensuring that leaders will not disobey Trump's wishes. Did I forget they also aim at getting rid of *"Marxist"* prosecutors? (McCarthy persecution of the fifties renewed?)

Steve Bannon revealed in an interview with British TV (LBC, Leading British Conversation) on January 23, 2024: *"We're training 3,000 people right now to step into the government on day one who don't need Senate confirmation. These are people with the populist MAGA America First agenda."*

Strong loyalty is, of course, an authoritarian requirement for their staff to remain securely in power. Loyalty meant so much to Hitler that the inscription over his door at Berchtesgaden read: "Meine Ehre heist Treue" ("My honor is loyalty"), the motto of the Nazi Party.

Revenge and retribution.

Trump has made clear his intentions for revenge and retribution against anyone he deems an enemy. *"I am your warrior. I am your justice. And for those who have been wronged and betrayed, I am your retribution,"* Trump declared at the Conservative Political Action Conference in March 2024.

Who are his targets? Those he believes have wronged him, include former Chairman of the Joint Chiefs of Staff General Milley, former Chief of White House Staff John Kelly, former Attorney General Jeff Sessions, former FBI Director Jim Comey, and others. Trump has stated on social media that he would appoint a special prosecutor to *"go after"* Biden, his family, and *"all others involved with the destruction of our elections, borders, & country itself."*

How? This can be possible through the control of loyal leaders in the Department of Justice. If unsuccessful via "normal channels and procedures, the possibility of invoking the Insurrection Act seems to have been discussed to help silence protests against him.[171]

On December 12, 2023, in his speech at a Young Republican Dinner, Gavin Wax, the club's 29-year-old president, said: *"Since I know the deep state is listening tonight, once President Trump is back in office, we won't be playing nice anymore. It will be a time for retribution. All those responsible for destroying our once-great country will be held to account after baseless years of investigations, government lies, and media lies against this man. Now it is time to turn the tables on these crooks and lock them up for a change."*

Trump, attending the dinner, replied: *"Gavin, that was an excellent speech. That was an excellent speech, wow."*

Representatives Susie Wiles and Chris LaCivita of the Trump campaign deny reports about the abuse of power: *"These reports about personnel and policies specific to a second Trump Administration are purely speculative and theoretical. Any personnel lists, policy agendas, or government plans published anywhere are merely suggestions,"* they stated. *"Likewise, all 2024 campaign policy announcements will be made by President Trump or members of his campaign team,"* they added. *"Policy recommendations from external allies are just that—recommendations."*

Rout out vermin: Trump adopting Hitler's policy.

At a rally on Veterans Day in mid-November 2023, Trump said, *"We pledge to you that we will rout out the communists, the Marxists, the fascists, and the radical left thugs that live like vermin within the confines of our country. Undocumented immigrants are poisoning the blood of our country."*

This echoes Hitler's 1934 rhetoric: *"If I can send the flower of the German nation into the hell of war without pity, then surely I have the right to remove millions of an inferior race that breeds like vermin,"* referring to the Jews. Hitler repeatedly referred to Jews as *"poisoning the bloodstream"* of the country.

Immigration: Deportation of immigrants on a large scale.

If these plans become reality, millions of illegal immigrants will be *"rounded up,"* placed temporarily in concentration camps, and then deported. According to Stephen Miller, Trump confirmed these intentions, stating, *"Following the Eisenhower model, we will carry out the largest domestic deportation operation in American history."*

To dispel doubts about their plans, Miller said, *"Any activists who doubt President Trump's resolve in the slightest are making a drastic error. Trump will unleash the vast arsenal of federal powers to implement the most spectacular migration crackdown. A vast number of American businesses will be targeted with workplace raids by immigration legal activists. "…The immigration legal activists won't know what's happening… It will be celebrated by American workers, who will now be offered higher wages with better benefits to fill these jobs."* [172]

But will this lead to higher wages for American workers? Previous studies on the economic effect of immigration show that the effects differ for high-skilled and low-skilled worker segments. In almost all cases studied, high-skilled immigration positively affects the long-term aspects of the economy. In many cases, low-skilled immigrants suppress local wages, but by relatively small amounts. Moreover, the demand for low-skilled workers in many regions is higher than the American workforce can meet.

Finish the wall.

About 450 miles (725 km) were built—for American taxpayers' money—during his first term, which was about a quarter (23%) of the 1,954-mile (3,145-km) borderline with Mexico. (about 400 of the 700 miles were replacement projects.) The cost has been estimated to be about $15 billion—and taken from military funds, as Congress did not approve the project. [173] Trump wants to complete the wall–no cost estimates revealed.

A radical move to the right on education.

Trump plans for more direct federal government control, firing *"radical left"* officials, removing diversity and
inclusion programs, and reducing tenure contracts for
teachers by rewarding schools that abolish tenure. This
means silencing critical thinking.

Increased military spending and expanding military use.

Trump proposes using the military against drug cartels
and street crime, with the next step being demonstrations.
Any authoritarian regime uses the military extensively to
maintain power.

Leaving NATO (North Atlantic Treaty Organization).

According to Commissioner Thierry Breton, Trump
told Ursula von der Leyen (President of the European
Commission) in a 2020 meeting, *"You have to understand. If
Europe is under attack, we are never going to help you. NATO
is dead. We are going to leave NATO. And by the way, you owe
'me' $400 million because you did not pay for your military
defense."* This would be great news for Putin, giving him
a boost to continue the invasion of Ukraine. No wonder
Russia (secretly) supports Trump in his fight to become
the U.S. president in 2024!

Pardoning most of the January 6, 2021, rioters.

Trump has said he wants to pardon nearly all of the convicted January 6 rioters (about 500 so far). This is within presidential powers and requires no judicial stretches or tricks. However, if done, it would show an apparent contempt for the law.

Strong support of Israel and *"Strongman"* Netanyahu.

Trump continues to show strong support for Israel and its leader, Benjamin Netanyahu.

Removing military aid to Ukraine.

Trump plans to take away the military aid that helps Ukraine resist Russia's invasion.

Maintaining restricted abortion rules imposed by the supreme court.

Trump has claimed credit for enabling the Supreme Court to limit women's abortion rights and appears content with a solution where each state decides the fate of abortion rights.

Artificial intelligence.

Trump plans to repeal President Joe Biden's recent executive order on artificial intelligence. This controversial order gave the government more insight and control over commercial companies developing AI systems and met significant opposition in Congress, particularly among Republicans. Tom Wheeler, former chairman of the Federal Communications Commission, sighed, *"The reality is, when you have a non-functional Congress, your choices are to either sit around and watch the boat sink … or to look for ways to make the boat move."*

Other conservative and right-wing measures: Gun freedom.

Trump advocates for unregulated gun ownership, aiming to undo all restrictions enacted by President Biden. *"Every single Biden attack on gun owners and manufacturers will be terminated my very first week back in office, perhaps my first day,"* Trump said in a recent speech at the Great American Outdoor Show in Harrisburg.

Gender issues.

Trump proposes removing Medicare support for gender-affirming care.

Housing grants.

Trump plans to eliminate housing grants initiated during the Obama era, aimed at areas affected by segregation and poverty.

A couple of rather *"lofty"* promises.

- Introduce baby bonuses to create a baby boom and design ten new "Freedom Cities" in the U.S.
- Broker a deal between Ukraine and Russia to end the war.

The authoritarian path of "project 2025".

The scariest and most democratically dangerous aspect of *"Project 2025,"* partly adopted and modified by Trump's team, is not just the list of conservative and far-right ideas and measures. These ideas have political support from many. The real threat lies in the authoritarian path toward a sovereign leader with complete control over a judiciary system without the independent power to stop or restrain his illegal activities.

Voices raised about the danger:

Jonathan Kaplan, November 20, 2023:

A journalist who has known Trump for nearly 30 years and author of "The Betrayal" says, *"Trump is more prone to break the rules of democracy now than he was when he first became President. He is angrier, leaning more toward revenge and retribution. That is not my judgment; he says it. I am not making a value judgment here; I only describe what he says. And importantly, there is now nobody around him to prevent him from damaging himself politically and the country. If Trump is elected, loyalty is the first and most important qualification for serving in the White House or any top official position in the various federal government agencies, not to the party politics, not to the American people, but to Donald Trump. Trump's entire focus is on Trump. 'I am going after people who are against me because they are after you, and I am standing in their way.' The 'come retribution' theme has become prevalent."*

Washington Post, November 6, 2023:

Trump has told advisers and friends that he wants the DOJ to investigate former officials and allies who have become critical of his time in office. He has also talked about using the DOJ to prosecute officials at the FBI and the DOJ, including John Kelly, Mark Milley, and Bill Barr. In a recent CNN interview, Barr suddenly switched back to supporting Trump, saying he would vote for Trump if he were the Republican candidate. (Scared of retribution?)

The New Yorker, November 9, 2023:

What would a second term with Donald Trump look like? Trump is running on a platform of Revenge, Retribution, and Constitution-termination.

David Jolly:

Attorney and former GOP, suggested in a TV interview that Trump would use an *"enemies list"* to seek revenge against critics as his allies sought to *"advance his personal autocratic interest as well as an ideology that is toxic."* [174]

Dagbladet, Norway's second largest newspaper:

About a possible second Trump term: "This is how Trump will make the world more dangerous:"

"-Out of NATO,

–10% customs,

–reverse positive environment measure,

–suppress media,

–shrink voter rights,

–dislike the power of justice or any institution he sees as against him being led by a man like Biden (who Trump describes as a man that is a wholly owned subsidiary of the Chinese Communist Party and his son who sniffs cocaine off the butts of hookers.)

Trump further has stated: *"Make no mistake about it, ladies and gentlemen: we are in a nation that is under attack from within."* [175]

A recipe for internal war and an isolated United States."

The Guardian, January 2024:

"Former officials say Trump's attacks threaten the rule of law. The ex-president has made increasingly conspiratorial and authoritarian broadsides against prosecutors pursuing him. Trump's vitriolic attacks on a special counsel and two state prosecutors, claim in part that the charges against him amount to "election interference." His chief goal in attacking Smith, whom he labeled a 'deranged lunatic,' and other prosecutors and judges is to delay his trials well into 2024, or until after the election."

The Atlantic Magazine, December 18, 2023:

In a special edition, The Atlantic warns about the dangers of Trump securing a second term, describing it as *"inviting the dark ages across the planet."* The magazine argues that Trump does not respect democratic ideals or norms and is focused on a presidency of revenge. His loyalty is not to the Constitution but to himself. The article emphasizes the importance of taking Trump at his word, noting that there will be no more adults in the room acting as a safety net, such as Rex Tillerson and James Mattis, former DOJ head Bill Barr, and former Chief of Staff John Kelly. All members of his previous Cabinet have expressed that he threatens democracy. New *"loyalists"* have emerged, including Stephen Miller, Rick Grenell, and Kash Patel.

The Writing is on the Wall!

Looking at history, we see that in countries where leaders have obtained autocratic powers, they have a terrible impact on their population, favoring no one but the few. The favored ones are often family, relatives, and wealthy individuals who can consolidate their power. Putin in Russia is a scary example, and Orban in Hungary is another. They have maneuvered themselves into positions where their actions are not controlled by law. Will the United States be next?

The newly released movie "Civil War" should remind us how a divisive leader can create havoc—Barbara Walter's book "How Civil Wars Start" explains the mechanisms behind civil unrest and conflict. The year 2024 will reveal whether Donald Trump succeeds, determining if America will remain a nation based on democratic principles or be stripped of the mechanisms that prevent authoritarian leaders from reigning.

CHAPTER 14

DONALD TRUMP'S MESSY LEGACY

H e has been like a bull in a china shop, knocking over everything in his path. Whether spewing hateful rhetoric, cozying up to Putin, or showing his contempt for the law by attacking judges and prosecutors, he has a way of getting under people's skin. His supporters essentially see him as a hero and a champion of their values, but to most Americans, his time on the political scene has created a mess.

One of the defining features of Trump's presidency was his willingness to test the norms and conventions of American politics. Whether he was attacking the media, undermining the independence of the judiciary, or using the power of the presidency and leadership of the Republican Party to enrich himself and his family, Trump seemed to have little regard for the principles that have long governed American democracy. It was as if he thought the rules didn't apply to him.

His attempts to delegitimize the courts of law will put a dark mark on his legacy. In particular, his rhetoric became hateful and threatening toward the representatives of the law.

Trump's response to the COVID-19 pandemic was marked by confusion and misinformation, from downplaying the severity of the virus to promoting unproven treatments and conspiracy theories. He disregarded expert advice and spread anti-vaccine sentiment, creating a slow-motion train wreck. How many more people could still be alive if it had been handled better?

Trump's embrace of white supremacist ideology was also controversial. From the so-called "Southern Strategy" to his cozying up to far-right groups like the Proud Boys, Trump seemed to have no problem using racism and xenophobia to appeal to his base. It was a dangerous game, further creating a hardened division among Americans.

Highly controversially, the Trump administration, from 2016 to 2020, shifted the focus from long-term climate-beneficial measures to short-term economic benefits. During his administration, nearly one hundred environmental rules and regulations from the Obama era aimed at improving the climate were reversed. International agreements on climate goals were canceled unilaterally. Instead, the Trump administration focused on stimulating industries reliant on fossil fuels and downplaying the importance of renewable energy.

His economic policy leaned toward isolationism and was equally controversial. He imposed trade barriers on China and sought to impose higher tariffs on European countries. His tax cuts for the wealthy and large corporations were executed, seemingly mostly *"under the radar"* and unnoticed by the middle class and the not-so-wealthy, who instead believe *"he fights for us."*

Catherin Thorbecke has taken a closer look at his economic policy in her book *"A Look at Trump's Economic Legacy."*[176] which did not live up to his campaign statement: *"I'll be the greatest jobs president that God ever created."* It started well, with increased jobs and growth in the stock market. However, when COVID-19 hit, Trump's lack of effective leadership became apparent. Economic experts say that the American economy suffered more than necessary because Trump failed in leadership during the COVID-19 pandemic, which aggravated the financial downturn, domestic policies that primarily benefited the wealthy, and international trade policies that hurt U.S. industry and alienated traditional trade allies.

The most significant mark on his legacy will undoubtedly be his refusal to accept the 2020 presidential election results and the subsequent January 6th insurrection, when a mob of Trump supporters stormed the Capitol in an attempt to overturn the election results. This shocking display of violence and hatred laid bare the deep divisions in American society. In the midst of all this, an intimidated Republican Party leadership let him continue breaking the rules.

Despite all his flaws, Trump has used his skills as a demagogue to build an almost cult-like, die-hard fanbase that worships the ground he walks on.

Trump's legacy is messy. His presidency was controversial, from his divisive rhetoric to his alleged ties to Russia. Many Americans were deeply troubled by his behavior in office, and his approval ratings remained consistently low throughout his tenure. The latest ranking poll (2024) by historians ranks Trump last among all 45 US presidents.[177]

The fact is, Trump's presidency left a lasting mark on American politics and society, not in a good way. His divisive rhetoric, disregard for the rule of law, and embrace of white supremacist ideology have all contributed to a growing polarization within American politics, leading to a climate of distrust and division that threatens the very foundations of American democracy.

Is there anything to be learned from these years with Trump? Perhaps the most important lesson is that words matter. The language we use and the ideas we embrace have real-world consequences, and we need to be mindful of the impact they can have on others.

It is time to recognize *"beyond reasonable doubt"* that the GOP leadership is most to blame for this mess, and it is very much up to them to initiate the process of rectification. If they can manage to do that, perhaps the best course for the Democratic Party leadership is to let the past be the past.

REFLECTIONS WHILE WORKING ON THIS BOOK

Germany, 1929-1945:

A man emerged with one wish: Power.

One strategy: Tell a colossal lie, keep repeating it, and people will eventually come to believe it.

He succeeded and brought horrendous warfare upon the world.

His name is Adolf Hitler.

The United States, 2020-?

A man emerged with one wish: Power.

One strategy: Tell a colossal lie, keep repeating it, and people will eventually come to believe it.

He succeeded in splitting a nation and laid the groundwork for an authoritarian state upon the American people.

His name is Donald Trump.

ENDNOTES

1   Koirale, Naresh, (2021, Feb 10) "America is no longer a beacon for democracy." The Statesman. People's Parliament Always in Session. https://www.thestatesman.com/opinion/america-no-longer-beacon-democracy-1502951254.html

2   Polychroniou, C.J. (2022, December 8) "Noam Chomsky: "We're on the Road to a Form of Neofascism." TRUTHOUT. https://truthout.org/articles/noam-chomsky-were-on-the-road-to-a-form-of-neofascism/

3   Ignazi, Piero "Neo-Fascism." European Center for Populism Studies. https://www.populismstudies.org/Vocabulary/neo-fascism/

4   Kehoe, Thomas D. (2020, September) "Thirteen Similarities Between Donald Trump and Adolf Hitler." Medium. https://tdkehoe.medium.com/thirteen-similaritites-between-donald-trump-and-adolf-hitler-3a97a8055dde

5   Ullrich, Volker, (2016, September 6) "Hitler: Ascent 1889–1939." Published by Knopf.

6   Hitler, Adolf, (1922) (1925) vol. 1, ch.10. Oxfordreference.com. https://www.oxfordreference.com/display/10.1093/acref/9780191843730.001.0001/q-oro-ed5-00005468

7   Langer, Walter C. "Adolf Hitler: Psychological Analysis of Hitler's Life & Legend." Office of Strategic Services, Jewish Virtual Library. Written with the collaboration of Prof. Henry A. Murr, Harvard Psychological Clinic; Dr. Ernst Kris, New School for Social Research; Dr. Bertram D. Lawin, New York Psychoanalytic Institute https://www.jewishvirtuallibrary.org/psychological-analysis-of-hitler-s-life-and-legend-2

8   Onion, Rebecca, (2016, May 18) "A 1942 List of Hitler's Lies."
     https://slate.com/human-interest/2016/05/a-list-of-hitlers-lies-
     compiled-by-the-office-of-war-information-in-1942.html
9   Dale, Daniel. (2021, Jan 16) "The 15 most notable lies of Donald
     Trump's presidency." CNN Politics.
     https://edition.cnn.com/2021/01/16/politics/fact-check-dale-
     top-15-donald-trump-lies/index.html
10   "Know about Adolf Hitler and his rise to power." Britannica.
     https://www.britannica.com/summary/Adolf-
     Hitler#:~:text=The%20economic%20slump%20of%20
     1929,invited%20him%20to%20be%20chancellor.
11   Kakutani, Michiko, (2016, Sept 27) "In 'Hitler,' an Ascent From
     'Dunderhead' to Demagogue"
     https://www.nytimes.com/2016/09/28/books/hitler-ascent-
     volker-ullrich.html
12   "A leader who makes use of popular prejudices and false claims
     and promises in order to gain power." For a more in-depth insight:
     "A Century of Demagogues in Europe" by Ivan T. Berend
13   Signer, Michael. From his book "Trump the demagogue."
14   Ullrich, Volker, (2016, September 6) "Hitler: Ascent 1889-1939."
     Published by Knopf.
15   Signer, Michael. From his book "Trump the demagogue."
16   CNN (2022, November) "Trump's tendency to blame everyone
     but himself." YouTube.
     https://www.youtube.com/watch?v=1BOW9c8A9lM
17   Gerstein, Josh. (2017, 15 February) "FBI releases files on Trump
     apartments' race discrimination probe in '70s."
     https://www.politico.com/blogs/under-the-radar/2017/02/
     trump-fbi-files-discrimination-case-235067
18   Lopoez, German. (2020, August 13) "Donald Trump's long history
     of racism, from the 1970s to 2020."
     https://www.vox.com/2016/7/25/12270880/donald-trump-
     racist-racism-history
19   "Adolf Hitler's wealth and income." Wikipedia.
     https://en.m.wikipedia.org/wiki/Adolf_Hitler%27s_wealth_and_
     income
20   WORTH REPEATING: Can't Happen Here?—PHAWKER.
     COM—Curated News, Gossip, Concert Reviews, Fearless

Political Commentary, Interviews….Plus, the Usual Sex, Drugs and Rock n' Roll.
https://phawker.com/2016/09/30/worth-repeating-cant-happen-here/

[21] Koessler, Maximilian "Nazi Justice and the Democratic Approach: The Debasement of Germany's Legal System." The New York Bar.

[22] Dictatorship 1, Democracy Nil—The People Loose—ACOMSDave.
https://acomsdave.com/dictatorship-1-democracy-nil-the-people-loose/

[23] Khalil, Mona. (2020, December 21) "President Trump's Attacks on the Rule of Law, From A to Z." Pass Blue Independent Coverage of the UN.
https://www.passblue.com/2020/12/21/president-trumps-attacks-on-the-rule-of-law-from-a-to-z/

[24] "Judische richter am Kammergericht nach 1933—eine dokumentation 27." Hans Bergemann & Simone Ladwig-Winters.

[25] "The History of the Pardon Power."
https:www.whitehousehistory.org/the-history-of-the-pardon-power

[26] Silverstein, Ken. (2000, Jan 6) "Ford and der Fuhrer." The Nation.
https://www.thenation.com/article/archive/ford-and-fuhrer/

[27] "Top Industries, federal election data for Donald Trump, 2020 cycle." Open. Secrets. (Based on Federal Election Commission data released electronically on 03/22/21.)
https://www.opensecrets.org/2020-presidential-race/donald-trump/industries?id=N00023864

[28] "Hitler Cabinet." Wikipedia.
https://en.wikipedia.org/wiki/Hitler_cabinet

[29] Gayle, Tina. (2021, September 21) "Hitler's Inner Circle: The 10 Most Powerful Men in Nazi Germany."
https://www.historyhit.com/hitlers-inner-circle/

[30] Reuters. (2021, January 16) "Trump's inner circle."
https://www.reuters.com/news/picture/trumps-inner-circle-idUSRTX8M67T

[31] "What happened to Michael Flynn?" The Atlantic, July 8, 2022.
https://www.theatlantic.com/ideas/archive/2022/07/michael-flynn-conspiracy-theories-january-6-trump/661439/

[32] "A Timeline of Paul Manafort's Career." The Atlantic, February 8, 2018
https://www.theatlantic.com/membership/archive/2018/02/a-timeline-of-paul-manaforts-career/552437/

[33] "Adolf Hitler | He's really different from all the others—Klara Hitler about her son" | Documentary. YouTube.
https://youtu.be/srEwOkLaoPE?si=RoGOs9HByCOOUBA8

[34] "Sturmabteilung, Storm Troopers, also known as "Brown Shirts. "The World Holocaust Remembrance Center.
https://www.yadvashem.org/odot_pdf/Microsoft%20Word%20-%205986.pdf

[35] Christopher S. Parker, professor of political science at the UW and co-author of the research.

[36] 1. Death threats to election workers:
"USA 2020/2021: Same wish and strategy. The man's name: Trump."
https://youtu.be/Jpg-OzYoKXw?si=5Z1qeg_IMhTbNhG3
2. "People Left Death Threats for Election Workers. We Called Them Back." YouTube January 11, 2022.
https://youtu.be/t3w5NuUsOq8
3. So, Linda. (2021, June 11) "Trump-inspired death threats are terrorizing election workers." Reuter investigates.
https://www.reuters.com/investigates/special-report/usa-trump-georgia-threats/

[37] Mary Trump. Ph.D. in clinical psychology from Adelphi University.
"Too Much and Never Enough: How My Family Created the World's Most Dangerous Man." Simon & Schuster, published 2020, July 14.

[38] Alfaro, Mariana (2018, December 27) "Donald Trump avoided the military draft 5 times, but it wasn't uncommon for young men from influential families to do so during the Vietnam War." Business Insider.
https://www.businessinsider.com/donald-trump-avoided-the-military-draft-which-was-common-at-the-time-vietnam-war-2018-12

[39] Villano, Steve. (2016, June 3) "The Trumps: "An Incestuous Intertwining with Organized Crime."

https://stevevillano.medium.com/the-trumps-an-incestuous-intertwining-with-organized-crime-ab65316c2b48

[40] Qiu, Linda. (2016, March 2) "Trump's business dealings with the mob or mob-related characters are widely documented." https://www.politifact.com/factchecks/2016/mar/02/ted-cruz/yes-donald-trump-has-been-linked-mob/

[41] D'Antonio, Michael. (2016, March 29) "The Men Who Gave Trump His Brutal Worldview." Politico. https://www.politico.com/magazine/story/2016/03/2016-donald-trump-brutal-worldview-father-coach-213750/ D'Antonio is also the author of Never Enough: Donald Trump and the Pursuit of Success, which was published by Thomas Dunne Books on November 22, 2015.

[42] New York Times Editorial Board. (2018, October 2) "Donald Trump and the Self-Made Sham. Now let's see your tax returns, Mr. President." https://www.nytimes.com/2018/10/02/opinion/donald-trump-tax-fraud-fred.html?auth=forgot-password&referring_pv_id=H0KgYetg-IP6nV7gxgwRd8An

[43] Gwenda Blair. "The Trumps: Three Generations of Builders and a Presidential Candidate." Published 2000.

[44] Alexander, Dan. (2023, October 23) "Here's How Much Donald Trump Is Worth." Forbes. https://www.forbes.com/sites/danalexander/article/the-definitive-networth-of-donaldtrump/?sh=29b0ea0b2a8e

[45] "S&P 500 Index—90 Year Historical Chart." Macrotrends. https://www.macrotrends.net/2324/sp-500-historical-chart-data

[46] How Trump Got Rich: The Real Story. https://www.youtube.com/watch?v=NUyicbdB07o

[47] "2016 U.S. Presidential Election—Statistics & Facts." Statista. https://www.statista.com/topics/2722/2016-election#dossier-chapter2

[48] "2016 Electoral College Results" https://www.archives.gov/electoral-college/2016

[49] Hanson, Victor Davis. (2016, November 11) "Why Trump Won." Hoover Institution. https://www.hoover.org/research/why-trump-won

50 Neven, Quentin (2018-2019) "Make Rhetoric Great Again: Donald Trump's communication strategies during the presidential elections of 2016." Liege University.
https://matheo.uliege.be/bitstream/2268.2/7556/4/Make%20Rhetoric%20Great%20Again.pdf

51 Libresco, Emily. (2018) "Dilbert on Trump." Brunswick Review, Issue 16, 2018.
https://www.brunswickgroup.com/media/4626/dilbert.pdf

52 Lamont, Michèle, Bo Yun Park, and Elena Ayala-Hurtado. 2017. "Trump's Electoral Speeches and His Appeal to the American White Working Class." British Journal of Sociology 68 (S1):S153–S180.
https://dash.harvard.edu/bitstream/handle/1/34864122/BJS_Trumps_Electoral_Speeches.pdf?sequence=1&isAllowed=y

53 Factcheck.org (2015, December 21) The 'King of Whoppers': Donald Trump
https://www.factcheck.org/2015/12/the-king-of-whoppers-donald-trump/

54 "I am a Popularist': A Critical Discourse Analysis of the Populist Rhetoric of Donald Trump's Presidential Campaign." Scholar Page.
http://hdl.handle.net/10125/70335

55 Haltiwanger, John. (2022, December 26) "Trump's biggest accomplishments and failures from his one-term presidency." Business Insider.
https://www.businessinsider.com/trump-biggest-accomplishments-and-failures-heading-into-2020-2019-12

56 "Political positions of Donald Trump."
Subsection: Politics and policies during presidency.
https://en.m.wikipedia.org/wiki/Political_positions_of_Donald_Trump

57 Birx Deborah. "Silent Invasion: The Untold Story of the Trump Administration, COVID-19, and Preventing the Next Pandemic Before It's Too Late." Harper Collins. Published April 2022.

58 Center on Budget and Policy Priorities. (2021, January 15) "The Trump Administration's Health Care Sabotage."
https://www.cbpp.org/research/health/the-trump-administrations-health-care-sabotage

59 According to many sources, incl. Pew Research survey published November 19, 2020: "The Trump era has seen a decline in America's global reputation."
https://www.pewresearch.org/fact-tank/2020/11/19/the-trump-era-has-seen-a-decline-in-americas-global-reputation/

60 Kessel, Hannah. (2022) "Backsliding: Donald Trump, Conspiracy Theory & Democratic Decline." Trinity College Digital Repository.
https://digitalrepository.trincoll.edu/theses/968/

61 Buchhholz, Katharina. (2020, October 2015) "Trump Administration Reversed 100 Environmental Rules." Infographic Newsletter.
https://www.statista.com/chart/18268/environmental-regulations-trump-administration/

62 Floyd, David. (2022, April 30) "Explaining the Trump Tax Reform Plan." By David Floyd.
https://www.investopedia.com/taxes/trumps-tax-reform-plan-explained/

63 A much-discussed special tax deduction. It gives owners of pass-through businesses (including sole proprietorships and partnerships) a 20% deduction for pass-through income.

64 Report. (2024, April 30) "The Tax Cuts and Jobs Act Failed To Deliver Promised Benefits" CAP20.
https://www.americanprogress.org/article/the-tax-cuts-and-jobs-act-failed-to-deliver-promised-benefits/#:~:text=The%20
2017%20law%20changes%20disproportionately,average%20tax%20cut%20of%20%2461%2C090.

65 Reality Check team, BBC News. (2020, November 3) "US 2020 election: The economy under Trump in six charts."
https://www.bbc.com/news/world-45827430

66 Dow jones industrial closing price gzdrp.
https://topoptionsdqdncmg.netlify.app/peightell66424cyhy/dow-jones-industrial-closing-price-seka.html

67 Millhiser, Ian. (2020, March 18) "The Dow Jones falls to where it was when Trump took office. More than three years of solid market returns evaporated in a few weeks, due to coronavirus."
https://www.vox.com/2020/3/18/21181976/dow-jones-trump-lower-coronavirus

68 Phan, Karena. (2022, April 13) "Inaccurate inflation figures circulate on social media." AP FACT CHECK.
https://apnews.com/article/fact-checking-112809830820

69 Rushe, Dominic. (2024, February 2) "Biden hails robust jobs market as proof US economy is "strongest in the world."
https://www.theguardian.com/business/2024/feb/02/us-jobs-report-january

70 Kiely, Eugene, Jackson, Brooks, and others. (2021, October 8) "Trump's Final NumbersStatistical indicators of President Trump's four years in office.
https://www.factcheck.org/2021/10/trumps-final-number

71 Neufeld, Dorothy. (2022, October 14) "Visualizing 40 Years of U.S. Interest Rates."
https://www.visualcapitalist.com/sp/visualizing-40-years-of-u-s-interest-rates/

72 Sloan, Allan and Podkul, Cezary. (20221, January 14) "Donald Trump Built a National Debt So Big (Even Before the Pandemic) That It'll Weigh Down the Economy for Years." ProPublica.
https://www.propublica.org/article/national-debt-trump

73 Narea, Nicole. (2022, November 29) "Donald Trump's long history of enabling white supremacy, explained."
https://www.vox.com/policy-and-politics/23484314/trump-fuentes-ye-dinner-white-nationalism-supremacy

74 Article. (October 29, 2020) "The Trump Administration Treats Seniors as Expendable"
https://www.americanprogress.org/article/trump-administration-treats-seniors-expendable/

75 Baker, Sam. (2024, February 19) "Historians rank Trump as worst president." Axios.
https://www.axios.com/2024/02/19/presidents-survey-trump-ranks-last-biden-14th

76 "Presidential Historians Survey 2021. C-Span.
https://www.c-span.org/presidentsurvey2021/?page=overall

77 "Presidential election, 2024."
https://ballotpedia.org/Presidential_election,_2024

78 Professor of history and Italian studies at New York University. Author of two books on fascism and two books on "strongmen," the latest of which is "Strongmen: How They Rise, Why They Succeed, How They Fall."

[79] Pape, Roberts. "The Chicago study on security and threats." https://youtu.be/dskVval50AE?si=NDfte6pAIi6H0DNA

[80] Farley, Robert. (2021, July 29) "Republicans' Shaky, No Evidence Attempt to Cast Blame on Pelosi for Jan. 6." Factcheck.org. https://www.factcheck.org/2021/07/republicans-shaky-no-evidence-attempt-to-cast-blame-on-pelosi-for-jan-6/

[81] Cheney, Kyle. (2022, February 15) "What the GOP meant when it called Jan. 6 'legitimate political discourse." https://www.politico.com/news/2022/02/15/gop-meaning-jan-6-legitimate-political-discourse-00008777

[82] Delusionist, a person who is prone to delusions, false beliefs that are not based on reality.

[83] Joscelyn, Tom, Eisen, Norman L. and Wertheimer, Fred. (2024, February 8)
"Dissecting Trump's "Peacefully and Patriotically" Defense of the January 6th Attack."
https://www.justsecurity.org/91904/dissecting-trumps-peacefully-and-patriotically-defense-of-the-january-6th-attack/

[84] Winberg, Oscar. (2017, July) "Insult Politics: Donald Trump, Right-Wing Populism, and Incendiary Language." European Journal of American Studies.
https://www.researchgate.net/publication/318880524_Insult_Politics_Donald_Trump_Right-Wing_Populism_and_Incendiary_Language

[85] Ben-Ghiat, Ruth. (Originally published July 2020) "Strongmen. Mussolini to the present."

[86] "List of nicknames used by Donald Trump."
https://en.m.wikipedia.org/wiki/List_of_nicknames_used_by_Donald_Trump

[87] Abutaleb Yasmeen and Paletta Damian. (2021, June 29) "Nightmare Scenario: "Inside the Trump Administration's Response to the Pandemic That Changed History." Amazon books.

[88] Bender, Michael C. (Published 2021, July 13) "Frankly, We Did Win This Election: The Inside Story of How Trump Lost."

[89] Quealy, Kevin, (2021, Jan 19) "The Complete List of Trump's Twitter Insults (2015-2021)."
https://www.nytimes.com/interactive/2021/01/19/upshot/trump-complete-insult-list.html

[90] Swaine, Jon and Adolphe, Juweek. (Updated 2019, August 29) "Violence in the name of Trump."
https://www.theguardian.com/us-news/ng-interactive/2019/aug/28/in-the-name-of-trump-supporters-attacks-database

[91] Phillips, Aleks. (2024, March 20) "Donald Trump Dementia Evidence 'Overwhelming,' Says Top Psychiatrist." Newsweek.
https://www.newsweek.com/donald-trump-dementia-evidence-overwhelming-top-psychiatrist-1881247

[92] Ulmer, Alexandra and Reid, Tim. (2024, February 14) "Do not read too much into Biden, Trump verbal stumbles, experts caution."
https://www.reuters.com/world/us/do-not-read-too-much-into-biden-trump-verbal-stumbles-experts-caution-2024-02-14/

[93] McLoughlin, Aoibheann. (2021, December 20) "The Goldwater Rule: a bastion of a bygone era?
https://www.ncbi.nlm.nih.gov/pmc/articles/PMC8886301/

[94] "The Dangerous Case of Donald Trump: 27 Psychiatrists and Mental Health Experts Assess a President." Edited by Jerome L. Kroll Journal of the American Academy of Psychiatry and the Law Online June 2018, 46 (2) 267-271;

[95] Norwegian word and origin: "SNILL:" To be kind. "SNILLISM:" To be overly kind and understanding for fear of making unpopular decisions.

[96] McNiff, S. and Roberts, S. (2023, May 31) "Some Narcissism Is A Good Thing. Here's Why." Where they cite from Ph.D. Craig Malkin's book "Rethinking Narcissism."

[97] Biggers, Larissa. (2022, December 15) "9 Signs of Narcissistic Personality Disorder. Narcissism vs. Narcissistic Personality Disorder."
https://www.dukehealth.org/blog/9-signs-of-narcissistic-personality-disorder

[98] Allen, Frances. (2017, Feb 14) "An Eminent Psychiatrist Demurs on Trump's Mental State. N.Y. Times.
https://www.nytimes.com/2017/02/14/opinion/an-eminent-psychiatrist-demurs-on-trumps-mental-state.html

[99] Burgo, Joseph, Ph.D., licensed clinical psychologist. (2015, August 14) "The Populist Appeal of Trump's Narcissism. Why Trump's narcissistic personality attracts disaffected voters." Psychology Today.

https://www.psychologytoday.com/intl/blog/shame/201508/
the-populist-appeal-trumps-narcissism

[100] Alford, Henry. (2015, November 11) Citations from the article
"Is Donald Trump Actually a Narcissist? Therapists Weigh In!
As his presidential campaign trundles forward, millions of sane
Americans are wondering: What exactly is wrong with this
strange individual? Now, we have an answer." By Henry Alford,
November 11, 2015.
https://www.vanityfair.com/news/2015/11/donald-trump-
narcissism-therapists

[101] Eddy, Bill. (2019, Jun 18) "Mental Health Pro: Trump's Narcissistic
& Sociopathic Traits." Podcast David Pakman Show. Bill is
Co-Founder and President of the High Conflict Institute and
author of the book "Why We Elect Narcissists and Sociopaths—
and How We Can Stop," YouTube.
https://youtu.be/L37F2mPFZ_Y?si=E1cnN3E4d3wXZl25

[102] Allen, Frances. (2017, Feb 14) "An Eminent Psychiatrist Demurs
on Trump's Mental State. N.Y. Times.
https://www.nytimes.com/2017/02/14/opinion/an-eminent-
psychiatrist-demurs-on-trumps-mental-state.html

[103] Porter, Tom. (2019, December 5) "350 health professionals sign a
letter to Congress claiming Trump's mental health is deteriorating
dangerously amid impeachment proceedings." Business Insider.
https://www.businessinsider.com/psychiatrists-submit-warning-
trumps-mental-health-deteriorating-2019-12

[104] Grande, Todd, Ph.D., Licensed professional counselor of mental
health. (2020, August 18) "Is Donald Trump a Narcissist? Insidious
Maladaptive Narcissism." YouTube:
https://youtu.be/HY16OQY21DE?si=LLr1wRydDPBCMYEUw

[105] Dr. Steven Hassan. (2021) "Former Cult Follower Describes How
President Trump Has Created a Cult Following." YouTube.
https://www.youtube.com/watch?v=pNdm6M8ctfo

[106] Lee, Bandy. (2022) "Top Psychiatrist SOUNDS ALARM on
Trump's Deteriorating Mental Fitness." Meidas interview. YouTube.
https://youtu.be/DREKGn4nPhQ?si=iw5lbEHloB94cU1B

[107] Glass, Leonard L., associate professor of psychiatry at Harvard
Medical School. (2023, June 16) "What Makes Trump Act That
Way? A Psychiatrist and a Psychologist Weigh In."

https://www.nytimes.com/2023/06/16/opinion/letters/donald-trump-behavior.html

[108] D'Antonio. (Published 2015, November 22) "Never Enough: Donald Trump and the Pursuit of Success." Thomas Dunne Books

[109] Abrams, Abigail (2019, April 18) "Here's What We Know So Far About Russia's 2016 Meddling."
https://time.com/5565991/russia-influence-2016-election/

[110] (2021, Nov 13th) "Vladimir Putin has shifted from autocracy to dictatorship and Russians across the country are feeling the heat." The Economist.
https://www.economist.com/briefing/2021/11/13/vladimir-putin-has-shifted-from-autocracy-to-dictatorship

[111] Russia Bars Antiwar Candidate in Election Putin Is All But Sure of Winning
https://www.nytimes.com/2024/02/08/world/europe/russia-presidential-election-explained.html

[112] Sky News journalist team (2024, March 16) "Poisonings, plane crashes and falls from windows: What happened to Putin's most vocal critics."
https://news.sky.com/story/poisoned-jailed-and-mysterious-fall-from-window-whats-happened-to-vladimir-putins-most-vocal-critics-13066825

[113] Carlin, Robert L. (2021, August 13) "The Real Lessons of the Trump-Kim Love Letters."
https://foreignpolicy.com/2021/08/13/north-korea-trump-kim-jong-un-love-letters-diplomacy-nuclear-talks/

[114] Scheiring, Gabor. (2024, March 7) "I watched Hungary's democracy dissolve into authoritarianism as a member of parliament – and I see troubling parallels in Trumpism and its appeal to workers." The Conversation.
https://theconversation.com/i-watched-hungarys-democracy-dissolve-into-authoritarianism-as-a-member-of-parliament-and-i-see-troubling-parallels-in-trumpism-and-its-appeal-to-workers-224930

[115] Press release. (2024, January 18): "The Hungarian government threatens EU values, institutions, and funds, MEPs say."
https://www.europarl.europa.eu/news/en/press-room/20240112IPR16780/the-hungarian-government-threatens-eu-values-institutions-and-funds-meps-say

[116] Nguyen, Thu. (2024 March 13) "The European Union's Hungary Problem." Internationale Politik Quarterly.
https://ip-quarterly.com/en/european-unions-hungary-problem

[117] Professor of history and Italian studies at New York University. Author of two books on fascism and two books on "strongmen," the latest of which is "Strongmen: How They Rise, Why They Succeed, How They Fall."

[118] Kessler, G., Rizzo, S. and Kelly M. (2019, January 21) "President Trump made 8,158 false or misleading claims in his first two years." Washington Post.
https://www.washingtonpost.com/politics/2019/01/21/president-trump-made-false-or-misleading-claims-his-first-two-years/

[119] LATEST FALSE FACT-CHECKS ON DONALD TRUMP. Politifact. The Poynter Institute.
https://www.politifact.com/factchecks/list/?speaker=donald-trump&ruling=false

[120] YouTube clip "I GOT WRITES" with JOHN WALDRON
https://youtu.be/QnJFjuNecS0?si=CBWhcRv5edehIzRV

[121] Probasco, Jim. (Updated 2023, February 28) "Who Was Charles Ponzi? What Did He Create? A profile of the infamous inventor of the scam that bears his name."
https://www.investopedia.com/who-is-charles-ponzi-5216783

[122] Tyson, Neil DeGrasse The Three Kinds Of Truths w/ Neil DeGrasse Tyson. YouTube Channel "Universe University.
https://youtu.be/Uod0STnJndM?si=ujFw1baSiQ0

[123] "Keep Tongue From Evil."
https://www.youtube.com/shorts/KUjENtUPL_E

[124] **Lawsuit:** A legal dispute between two or more parties.
Civil lawsuits are legal disputes that arise when individuals have differing views on their legal obligations towards each other. The most common outcome of a civil lawsuit is monetary compensation.
Criminal lawsuits, however, involve specific crimes (misdemeanors and felonies.) In criminal cases, punishment is either prison, fine, or both.
Litigation: The formal process of filing a lawsuit or defending against one in court.
Misdemeanor: A misdemeanor is a type of offense punishable under criminal law. It is typically punishable by less than

12 months in jail. Community service, probation, fines, and imprisonment for less than a year are commonly issued punishments for misdemeanors.

Felony: A felony is a serious crime, often involving violence, that is considered more severe than a misdemeanor. It is typically punishable by imprisonment for more than one year or even death.

[125] Graham, David A. (2024, February 8) "The Cases Against Trump: A Guide."
https://www.theatlantic.com/ideas/archive/2024/02/donald-trump-legal-cases-charges/675531/

[126] "Litigation Tracker; Pending Criminal and Civil Cases against Donald Trump."
https://www.justsecurity.org/75032/litigation-tracker-pending-criminal-and-civil-cases-against-donald-trump/

[127] A Sisyphus task: Used to describe a task that can never be completed. In Greek mythology, the myth says that Sisyphus was set to roll a heavy stone for eternity as punishment for cheating death.

[128] Penzenstadler, Nick, and many others. (Donald Trump: Three decades 4,095 lawsuits."
https://www.usatoday.com/pages/interactives/trump-lawsuits/

[129] Boser, U., Schwaber, D. and Johnson S. (2017, March 30) "Trump University: A Look at an Enduring Education Scandal
https://www.americanprogress.org/article/trump-university-look-enduring-education-scandal/

[130] "Police officer lawsuits pile up against Trump over January 6
https://www.politico.com/news/2022/01/04/police-officer-lawsuits-capitol-riot-trump-526491

[131] Benen, Steve. (2024, March 20) "Trump scrambles in the hopes of delaying his Jan. 6 civil cases."
https://www.msnbc.com/rachel-maddow-show/maddowblog/trump-scrambles-hopes-delaying-jan-6-civil-cases-rcna144295

[132] Lander, Olivia. (2022, September 09) "Trump: I could declassify documents by thinking about it." Politico.
https://www.politico.com/news/2022/09/21/trump-i-could-declassify-documents-by-thinking-about-it-00058212

[133] Kimmel, Jimmy (2022, Feb 11) YouTube.
https://youtu.be/iSXSIQWQChs?si=XBn3-cnXy4vsQ0aM

134 Aftergut, Dennis and Tribe, Laurence H. (20224, January 16) "Judge Aileen Cannon Is Quietly Sabotaging the Trump Classified Documents Case." Slate. https://slate.com/news-and-politics/2024/01/judge-aileen-cannon-trump-classified-sabotage.html

135 Kirchner, Glenn. (2024) "Judge Aileen Cannon sets NO TRIAL DATE in Trump's classified documents/obstruction/espionage case." YouTube video. https://youtu.be/_h_GaHyKkyI?si=RQZ2J8sLlpOZxLVF

136 Graham, David A. (2023, August 1) "Trump Attempted a Brazen, Dead-Serious Attack on American Democracy. And now he's been indicted for it." The Atlantic. https://www.theatlantic.com/ideas/archive/2023/08/trump-indicted-january-6-jack-smith/674886/

137 Ramani S Durvasula. American clinical psychologist "Holding narcissists accountable, the DARVO method." YouTube: https://youtu.be/jPGrxHEcnp8?si=lqSlKZ_qf9-LjfQp

138 Donald Trump's Attacks On Our Democracy: Pt. 2—Trump's Attacks On Our Judicial System | Robin Messing. https://themessinglink.com/TrumpAttacksTheCourts

139 Feuer, Alan and Savage, Charlie. (2024, February 6) "Federal Appeals Court Rejects Trump's Claim of Absolute Immunity." Courthouse News Service. https://www.nytimes.com/2024/02/06/us/politics/trump-immunity-appeals-court.html

140 From Wikipedia: "Pleading the Fifth." A colloquial term often used to invoke the self-incrimination clause when witnesses decline to answer questions where the answers might incriminate them. https://en.m.wikipedia.org/wiki/Fifth_Amendment_to_the_United_States_Constitution

141 A civil investigation case by the New York State to explore whether "Trump's annual financial statements inflated the values of Trump's assets to obtain favorable terms for loans and insurance coverage, while also deflating the value of other assets to reduce real estate taxes."

142 "Trump sues New York attorney general in latest fight over business fraud claims." The Guardian, November 3, 2022. https://www.theguardian.com/us-news/2022/nov/03/trump-sues-letitia-james-ny-attorney-lawsuit

[143] (2020, February 14) "In His Own Words: The President's Attacks on the Courts." Brennan Center for Justice. https://www.brennancenter.org/our-work/research-reports/his-own-words-presidents-attacks-courts

[144] (2023, October 5) "A catalogue of Trump's attacks on judges, prosecutors, and witnesses." Washington Post. https://www.washingtonpost.com/politics/2023/10/05/catalogue-trumps-attacks-judges-prosecutors-witnesses/

[145] Rose, Ashtin. (2021, January 4) "YOU CAN CALL HER MADAM DA; FANI WILLIS ON MAKING HISTORY AS FULTON COUNTY'S FIRST WOMAN DISTRICT ATTORNEY." South Atlanta Magazine. https://fultoncountyga.gov/news/2021/01/04/you-can-call-her-madam-da-fani-willis-on-making-history

[146] Levine, Mike. (2020, May 30)" 'No Blame?' ABC News finds 54 cases invoking 'Trump' in connection with violence, threats, alleged assaults." ABCNews. https://abcnews.go.com/Politics/blame-abc-news-finds-17-cases-invoking-trump/story?id=58912889

[147] Maryann Trump. Earned a master's in public law and government from Columbia University in 1962. At the time of her retirement, she worked as an appellate federal judge in New Jersey. She died in 2023 at the age of 86.

[148] From different interviews. Here from a CNN interview Jan 31, 2024. https://youtu.be/K9D9igrRTA0?si=jChfB8gI088frYub

[149] Illarionov, Andrei. (December 2023) "I Worked with Putin: Here's What You Don't Know About Him." Interviewed by Jason Jay Smart, Kyiv Post. https://youtu.be/X2AwAXcScds?si=UKjav81jWU94HgkL Illarionov's credentials: Ph.D. in macroeconomics from St. Petersburg University in 1987. From 1993 to 1994, Illarionov served as chief economic adviser to the prime minister of the Russian Federation, Viktor Chernomyrdin. He resigned in February 1994 to protest changes in the government's economic policy. In July 1994, Illarionov founded the Institute of Economic Analysis and became its director. Illarionov has co-authored several economic programs for Russian governments and has written three books and more than 300 articles on Russian economic and social policies. From

2000 to December 2005, he was the chief economic adviser of Russian President Vladimir Putin and the president's personal representative in the G-8. At the end of 2005, he resigned and became an outspoken critic of Putin and the Kremlin. He is one of Russia's most forceful and articulate advocates of an open society and democratic capitalism. Andrei Illarionov was a senior fellow at the Cato Institute's Center for Global Liberty and Prosperity from 2006 to 2021. Since April 2021, he is a senior fellow at the non-governmental organization Center for Security Policy, Washington D.C

[150] American journalist and business book author who is best known for ghostwriting Trump: The Art of the Deal.

[151] Julia Loffe, Russian-American journalist. (2023, Jan 31) Interview with Frontline PBS:—"Putin and the Presidents."
https://www.youtube.com/watch?v=qEu0oRajJxE

[152] Clip from an article in Dagbladet, a nationwide Norwegian newspaper:
https://www.dagbladet.no/meninger/store-ego-sma-sko/76612911

[153] Smith, Gregory A. (2024, March 15) "5 facts about religion and Americans' views of Donald Trump." PEW Research.
https://www.pewresearch.org/short-reads/2024/03/15/5-facts-about-religion-and-americans-views-of-donald-trump/#:~:text=Among%20religious%20groups%2C%20White%20evangelical,very%20favorable%20opinion%20of%20him.

[154] "Pew Research Center political typology."
https://en.wikipedia.org/wiki/Pew_Research_Center_political_typology

[155] Cerda, Andy. (2023, July 21) "Little change in Americans' views of Trump over the past year."
https://www.pewresearch.org/short-reads/2023/07/21/little-change-in-americans-views-of-trump-over-the-past-year/

[156] Trump Trademarks "MAKE AMERICA GREAT AGAIN"—Stites & Harbison.
https://www.stites.com/resources/trademarkology/6023/

[157] Harte, Julia, Parker, Ned, Kahn, Chris, Eisler, Pete. (2019, October) "What MAGA means to Trump voters." REUTERS GRAPHICS.
https://fingfx.thomsonreuters.com/gfx/editorcharts/USA-ELECTION-TRUMP-MAGA/0H001BBVZ2XL/index.html

158 Joscely, Tom, Eisen, Norman L., and Wertheimer, Fred. (2024, February 8) "Dissecting Trump's "Peacefully and Patriotically" Defense of the January 6th Attack" https://www.justsecurity.org/91904/dissecting-trumps-peacefully-and-patriotically-defense-of-the-january-6th-attack/

159 Blake, Aaron. (2023, August 23) "7 ways MAGA Republicans differ from other Republicans." Washington Post. https://www.washingtonpost.com/politics/2023/08/22/maga-republicans-analysis/

160 New nationwide survey shows MAGA supporters' beliefs about the pandemic, the election and the insurrection | UW News. https://www.washington.edu/news/2021/02/05/new-nationwide-survey-shows-maga-supporters-beliefs-about-the-pandemic-the-election-and-the-insurrection/

161 MacWilliams, Matthew, Ph.D. (2016, January 17), "The One Weird Trait That Predicts Whether You're a Trump Supporter. And it's not gender, age, income, race or religion." Politico Magazine. A national poll in December 2015 sampling 1,800 registered voters across the country and the political spectrum. https://www.politico.com/magazine/story/2016/01/donald-trump-2016-authoritarian-213533/

162 Blum, Rachel M., and Parker, Christopher S. (2020/2021) "Panel Study Of The MAGA Movement." https://sites.uw.edu/magastudy/

163 Bowmann, Bridget. (2023, April 25) "'MAGA movement' widely unpopular, new poll finds." https://www.nbcnews.com/meet-the-press/meetthepressblog/maga-movement-widely-unpopular-new-poll-finds-rcna81200

164 Study.com https://study.com/learn/lesson/cult-characteristics-types-behavior.html

165 Lee, Bandy. (2021, January 11) "The 'Shared Psychosis' of Donald Trump and His Loyalists." Scientific American. https://www.scientificamerican.com/article/the-shared-psychosis-of-donald-trump-and-his-loyalists

166 Hassan, Steven, "The Cult of Trump: A Leading Cult Expert Explains How the President Uses Mind Control." Free Press. Published September 1, 2020.

[167] Eddy, Bill. (2021, January 8) "The Trump Bubble Bursts: It's Personality, Not Politics. High-conflict politicians have a predictable and dangerous pattern." Psychology Today. https://www.psychologytoday.com/intl/blog/5-types-people-who-can-ruin-your-life/202101/the-trump-bubble-bursts-its-personality-not

[168] "Building *now* for a conservative victory through policy, personnel, and training." https://www.project2025.org

[169] Cai, Sophia. (2023, May 21) "Trump's vision, revealed." Axios, Politics & Policy. https://www.axios.com/2023/05/21/trump-2025-vision

[170] Katz, Eric. (2022, July 22) "If Trump Is Reelected, His Aides Are Planning to Purge the Civil Service." https://www.govexec.com/workforce/2022/07/trump-reelected-aides-plan-purge-civil-service/374842

[171] Samuels, Brett. (2023, November 16) "Trump signals he's out for revenge in second term." https://thehill.com/homenews/campaign/4311194-trump-signals-revenge-in-second-term/

[172] Reinert, Kenneth A. (2023, December 12) "MAGA gets the economics of immigration all wrong." The Hill. https://thehill.com/opinion/immigration/4355506-maga-gets-the-economics-of-immigration-all-wrong/

[173] Valverde, Miriam. (2020, July "Donald Trump promised to build a border wall and make Mexico pay for it. That didn't happen." Politifact. https://www.politifact.com/truth-o-meter/promises/trumpometer/promise/1397/build-wall-and-make-mexico-pay-it/

[174] Lee, Moran. (2023, Nov2) "Ex-GOP Congressman Spitballs Truly Chilling Scenario Of Second Trump Term." Huffington Post. https://www.huffpost.com/entry/david-jolly-donald-trump-second-term_n_65438258e4b06bc01e23150e

[175] Lillegaard, Henning. (2024, January 30) "Slik vil Trump gjøre verden farligere." https://www.dagbladet.no/nyheter/slik-vil-trump-gjore-verden-farligere/80839154

176 Thorbecke, Catherine. (2021, January 20) "A look at Trump's economic legacy. Examining the outgoing president's policies from tax cuts to trade wars." ABC news.
https://abcnews.go.com/Business/trumps-economic-legacy/story?id=74760051

177 Baker, Sam. (2024, February 19) "Historians rank Trump as worst president." Axios.
https://www.axios.com/2024/02/19/presidents-survey-trump-ranks-last-biden-14th

Made in the USA
Columbia, SC
29 May 2025